SUCCESS BLAST

How To Succeed, Triumph, Thrive & Skyrocket To Career & Business Success!

Jack Alan Levine

GREAT
HOPE
PUBLISHING
Coconut Creek, Florida

WHAT THEY ARE SAYING!

"This is it. A book that finally gives honest, real-world advice on what it takes to work hard, to fight for what you want, and succeed big. I'm already a well-read, successful Merrill Lynch executive and within the first few pages I simply HAD to start taking notes on all the powerful, creative ideas and inspiring stories that Jack Levine shares in these pages. Get this book, and get your pen and note pad ready, because this book will Blast you up to a whole new level!"
Aaron W. Kassler, CIMA® CPFA CRPC®,
Merrill Lynch Wealth Management
Vice President & Senior Financial Advisor

"Wow! What a tremendous contribution Jack has made to us through his new book. My only regret is that I didn't have these nuggets of wisdom earlier in my business life. What I love is the way Jack articulates from personal experience time-proven business success principles. Just the "Take Action" ideas at the end of each chapter will transform your life and business. I can't wait to see the incredible results I get as I continue to apply the content in this book!"
Jim Collins
Author of Beyond Positive Thinking and
The Secret to Abundant Living

"Definitely goes on top of my list of Great Business Books! Great career insights packed into a very fun read. A book I will not stop referring back to."
Andre Kursancew
RBC Capital Markets Director of Mergers and Acquisitions
Deutsche Bank Former Director VP Mergers and Acquisitions

"I wish I would of had this information at the start of my career... Great Advice! Read it and use this powerful tool!"
Mark W. Koch
Prelude Pictures, Chairman

"Jack's advice to my students in the College of Business has helped launch many successful careers in a variety of industries. The business, marketing, management and entrepreneurial students that Jack spoke to were mesmerized by his passion, experience, knowledge and encouragement, but most of all they were blown away as they received from Jack the education of a lifetime! Now you can have it too... read *Success Blast*, it's the best investment in your career or business you could ever make! You won't be sorry!"

Joseph Patton
Management Professor at Florida Atlantic University
Former Management Professor at University of Miami

"Jack Levine does a masterful job of laying out a pathway for success for anyone that wants to pursue a career in business. *Success Blast* is inspirational and motivating. As a 35 year executive in the private sector, I highly recommend this book for individuals of all ages. Well done Jack!

Buck Martinez
Senior Director Project Development at FPL (Florida Power & Light) and Founder and President Student ACES

"Mix together your own perseverance with a highly successful and deeply wise guide and you cannot fail. Jack Alan Levine – and his newest, wonderful book, *Success Blast* – is your guide! I deeply trust Jack, and love this book!"

Dr. John Stahl-Wert
Founder and Owner, Newton Institute
Internationally Bestselling Author, *The Serving Leader*

"Jack's book is your SOS (secrets of success) for career and business success".

Ray Holden
Miller's Ale House President/COO

SUCCESS BLAST

By Jack Alan Levine

Published by Great Hope Publishing LLC, Coconut Creek, Florida

Cover Design & Layout By Scott Wolf

www.JackAlanLevine.com
www.Don'tBlowItWithGod.com
www.LifeSolutionSeminars.com

E-mail: Jack@JackAlanLevine.com

ISBN – 978-0-9904097-8-6   Paperback
ISBN – 978-0-9904097-9-3   E-Pub

Library of Congress Control Number: 2018910436

Dedication

I want to thank all of you wonderful young professionals who let me pour into your lives and gave me the privilege and opportunity to share with you, mentor, encourage and instill some of the lessons I learned. I hope they have been and continue to be of value to you. I am so grateful for the opportunity to do so and get to know you, to spend time with you and watch you grow and develop. You have no idea how much this has blessed me. Thank you all.

TABLE OF CONTENTS

Introduction IX

Chapter 1:   Your Path To Success 15

Chapter 2:   Know What Motivates You 21

Chapter 3:   Enjoy The Ride 25

Chapter 4:   Work Smart 35

Chapter 5:   Differentiate Yourself 47

Chapter 6:   Understand the Future Value Of Experience 59

Chapter 7:   Make It Happen 65

Chapter 8:   Stay Relevant 71

Chapter 9:   Keep It Real 81

Chapter 10:   Look For Every Angle 91

Chapter 11:   Stay In The Game 97

Chapter 12:   Prepare To Win 103

Chapter 13:   Attitude 113

Chapter 14:   Take Time To Understand People 119

Chapter 15:   Seek Good Counsel 123

Chapter 16:   Do It The Right Way 135

Chapter 17:   Build A Smart Team 141

Chapter 18:   Overcoming Hidden Objections 147

Chapter 19:   The Most Important Lessons Ever 157

Ending Thoughts/Special Thanks 171

INTRODUCTION

My goal in writing this book is to give you practical business, career and leadership applications, discuss a few valuable lessons I've learned, and outline some things that worked... and others that didn't. I will walk you through my career and point out the critical things you need to know to succeed in business because that's really what it's all about—and not just succeeding, but getting ahead and doing it quicker. Some of these are life lessons while others pertain to personality and character, but all of them are critical. When combined, I believe you will be well on your way to business and career success greater than you ever imagined.

This book applies to people already in business as well as those just starting out. Each chapter begins with a "Snapshot" section, quickly highlighting the valuable lessons you will learn, and ends with a "Take Action" section, helping you process the information to take immediate action toward your personal success.

I have been so blessed and privileged to put many of the life and business lessons I've learned into action. It brings me great joy and satisfaction to teach them and mentor others along the way. I've had the opportunity to do this for decades. In my advertising, TV production and other businesses, I was able to mentor and help many young professionals improve their lives and careers. I want to encourage you to take the opportunity to do the same.

I had the privilege of watching many of them become highly successful and functioning executives and business people. I've also had the opportunity to share my knowledge and experience with many business and professional people in most of the ventures I've been associated with through the decades, including many of our entrepreneurial projects and companies we've managed, owned or invested in. These included partners, employees, vendors, clients, customers and people that I've come to know. I've also met and

I believe impacted positively many in church and the nonprofit world through charitable and worthwhile organizations and causes that I've been involved with.

It was very rewarding for me personally to have so many of them come back and thank me for the lessons I'd taught them. To this day I still have the blessing and honor of having them remind me of the value of a quote, lesson, advice, input, help or a potential solution to a problem I offered them at that specific time and place in their lives when they needed it most.

Many share how that wisdom stayed with them through their lives and helped them in other situations. They now pass it on and share it. Personally, I can think of no greater thrill. This must be what it's like for the musician to hear the applause of the crowd, or what the athlete experiences when the crowd goes wild cheering for his success. Or perhaps the look of admiration a great surgeon gets when he performs a lifesaving surgery. I usually smile as I remind myself of where and how specifically I learned those lessons and who taught them to me! I share many of those with you in this book.

I believe in order to keep it, you've got to give it away... and that's what we should be doing with all our knowledge, wisdom and experience. Sharing it with others so they can be blessed as it was shared with us.

It seems to me that people everywhere are hungry for wisdom. You can't just go out and scream "I have wisdom." It's not something you advertise. You earn the right to share what you know. I don't say this with pride, but I believe people can see it in you and know that your wisdom is something they desire. Much like the cool person you wish you were like. Or the rich person you see and say, "Hey! How can I get that. I want to be like that too."

With a successful person, you seek their knowledge and wisdom—whether it's in love, parenting, business, marriage, life, philosophy, physical health, spiritual or financial well-being. We all want the answers! We all want the keys to the universe... the secret to success! However, we don't want a ton of BS thrown at us. We don't want some self-serving creep shouting about how great he is. No don't tell me how great you are... teach me how I can be great!

I am extremely grateful to those people who poured into my life and taught me so much—many of whom I talk about in this book. I hope I gave them the same joy and gratitude I've received from those I've helped. What a privilege and joy to live long enough to see others come back and thank me for pouring into their lives.

So, I believe you will benefit no matter which side of the spectrum you're on when you're reading this book, if you are learning and seeking knowledge, I hope this book inspires you to go and get the knowledge and wisdom you need to succeed. If you already have it, by all means share it, teach it, live it, be it. Let others see it in you... I know you will be blessed.

Jack Hender

Jack

P.S. I know a lot of times in the book I use the pronoun "he" to reference a person, but the book applies to men and women equally. There is not meant to be any prejudice in that regard. It just wrote it that way for ease and convenience.

CHAPTER 1

YOUR PATH TO SUCCESS

SNAPSHOT

1. Discover why this book will help you succeed—whether you have been in business, have an established career or are just starting out.

2. Learn how to accurately choose the right path for your success based on your personality, giftedness and experience.

3. Understand the importance of being where the action is.

Of course, one of the first decisions you need to make in business is to choose your path to success. Are you an entrepreneur? Or do you want to be in the corporate world?

For example, you can go to work for a corporation, and you'll follow their rules and procedures and try to grow through their ranks. You'll have people above you telling you what to do and will be judged accordingly, constantly evaluated on your performance.

There are many advantages to the corporate world as an employee. You are usually working for a company with tremendous resources that can give you support, offer you benefits, and afford to pay other people to work with you and for you. Thus, the problems of the business are not necessarily your personal problems.

However, you are limited in what you can earn and how far you up the ranks you can go. Not to say this isn't a great opportunity. It can also be an amazing learning realm. I would definitely suggest starting out by working for a company — the bigger the better, for a lot of reasons.

A bigger company inherently has more people to like you. If you work for a single guy or a small firm where his family members are in the firm with him, you may get a lot of hands-on experience, and there's value to that. But first, there's no place to grow with the company. And second, you are limited to just the few people in the company to help you.

If you work for a larger company like Coca Cola or, as I did on Madison Avenue, a big company then known as NW Ayer Advertising that had 1,100 employees, you have an opportunity for a lot more people to like you and help you advance your career. We'll discuss this more, but I cannot stress to you the impact of having people in your life who want to advance your career. They can leap frog your career by years and get you on a path that you would have never been on otherwise. You want to expose yourself to those opportunities as frequently as possible.

I would say you are better off working in a janitor or assistant position at a large, major company in New York, Chicago, or LA than you are working in an executive position in a small market like Topeka, Kansas, or Syracuse, New York. Why? Because those markets are not where the action is happening. You may have the position and the job title, but you're not in a market where you can grow. If you want to be a movie actor, you go to Hollywood. If you want to be in advertising, you go to Madison Avenue or Los Angeles. If you want to be a stage actor, you go to Broadway.

Why do you think actors work as waiters and waitresses in New York City, looking for their big break on Broadway? They could remain the stars in small markets in some regional theater, but they know that's not their goal or dream. So the first point is—be where the action is.

Is there ever an advantage to starting your career in a small market? One of my friends, Dave Salomone, VP of one of the most well known cable networks in the world told me this: "There are advantages to small market jobs because they give you the ability to do more things." At twenty-three years old in Rochester, New York, he was directing baseball games for television broadcasts. By the time he got to the big markets, he had more hands-on experience than others.

That philosophy works if you use it as a quick stepping stone to get to the big markets and you get there quickly. However, you have to be very careful that you don't get pigeon-holed. You could start out in the media library, but you don't want to be the guy who stays there for five years. You need to be tugging on the shirt sleeve of writers, editors, and camera guys, saying, "Can I see what you're doing? Can I try it? Can you teach me?" You need to take an active role in moving forward and accelerating your career or you will get pigeon-holed.

When I graduated college, I began looking for work, but at that time there were no jobs in advertising. I had a degree (actually two degrees, advertising and sociology as I majored in both) from one of the best advertising schools in the country, the S.I. Newhouse School of Public Communications at Syracuse University. But the economy was tough, and there were no jobs to be found. I was a little discouraged that I wasn't able to find one right away. But my father encouraged me to hang in there, giving me another of the many great life lessons he would share with me. He told me, "Listen, it only takes one person to say yes." He said everybody in the world doesn't have to find a job, just you, and just one guy has to say yes to give you a chance.

That philosophy was accurate. Dad was a genius in that regard, and many others as well, and I did get the opportunity when one lady said yes. I went to work for NW Ayer Advertising. When I interviewed with their in-house human resources director, she said she couldn't hire me. I asked why. She said I was overqualified because the job I was applying for was a typist even though I had a college education. Why would I do that? For the very same reason I told you—I needed to be where the action was. I knew one thing for sure, if I could just get the door to open a crack, I would be able to kick it down. But I had to get it open.

So, I said to her, "Listen, if I'm overqualified, then aren't you guys getting a bargain for your money? Aren't the dollars you're spending for an employee going further?"She said, "Yes, but you're going to get bored and leave this position as soon as something else comes along." I said, "Look, I give you my word I will stay at this job for at least one year. In which case you are getting tremendous value for your money." She agreed with that, hired me and gave me my chance. Within three months she had promoted me internally, and my career was taking off like a rocket on Madison Avenue. I worked on some major campaigns of the time including AT&T "Reach Out and Touch Someone" and the US Army "Be All You Can Be."

So, remember, it only takes one person to say yes, you want to be where the action is, and you want to be around people who can help you leapfrog your career. That is the corporate side.

Let's talk about being an entrepreneur. When you're an entrepreneur you're your own boss, you make the rules, you lead the battle charge, and you run the ship. But also when you're leaving the office at the end of the day, the weight of the world is on your shoulders. That can be a positive in a couple of scenarios:

1. If you can handle the pressure and don't like to be stifled and working under corporate rules and regulations.

2. Your upside potential for earnings is unlimited because you're the boss.

I have done both. I have been in the corporate world and seen its benefits, and I have been an entrepreneur. I believe being an entrepreneur is much more fun with more upside, but it is not for everybody. You first have to understand your personality type and where you thrive. It does you no good to be an entrepreneur if you can't take the pressure and you don't like the roller coaster rides—physically, financially and emotionally—that you'll encounter running a business. It does you no good to be an entrepreneur if you're not a leader, or a visionary, or willing to work twenty-four/seven to do whatever it takes to get the job done.

I can't tell you how long it will take for you to succeed, but I can tell you if you apply the principles we're about to discuss, you will succeed—hopefully sooner than later.

TAKE ACTION

- Decide who you are. Are you an entrepreneur or a corporate person? Which path to success best aligns with your personality, giftedness and experience at this moment in time?

- Ask others who know you and whose opinion you value where they think you would thrive.

- Go where the action is. If you start small, plan to move up quickly. It's better to be a small fish in the huge pond where you want to be than a big fish in a small pond where you don't want to be. Plan to grow big once you're in the big pond!

- Kick down the barriers that hold you back. Take whatever job they'll let you have to get to work where you want to be. Overqualified? Make them an offer to take you they can't refuse. Then run with it. Underqualified? Get qualified, and show them you're willing to learn on the job at little cost to them. It will more than pay off in the long run.

CHAPTER 2

KNOW WHAT MOTIVATES YOU

> **SNAPSHOT**
>
> 1. Learn how your attitude toward money will impact your level of success.
>
> 2. Discover the importance of learning necessary lessons along the path to success.
>
> 3. Understand why being unique in business is critical to your success.

I believe money equals freedom. It is one of the things that drives me. I want to make money for that reason. That wasn't always the case... as a teenager I wanted money to buy stuff, but I had a different perception of money back then. As I got a little older, I realized I wanted money because it provided me freedom to do what I wanted. Here's why.

I hate to be told what to do. It bothers me. I can't stand it. I don't know why, but I've been that way since I was a little kid. I hated when the bell rang in school to go to the next class because I felt like cattle being herded from one place to the other. I always resented it, rebelled against it, and looked for a way out of that—in school, in business, and in life.

In school the way out was to graduate a year early. I always wanted to get someplace quicker, if possible, without forfeiting any of the benefit and experience I learned or earned along the way. That is a critical point. It's no good to get to someplace quicker if you don't learn what you're supposed to know.

I graduated high school a year early. I skipped twelfth grade not because I was so smart but by simply taking two additional classes instead of lunch and study hall. That got me the credits I needed. So, there was a way to get what I wanted, a loophole.

You're going to see this strategy as we move forward in business as well. We want to accomplish the same thing to get where we're going quicker. We don't want to sink down to the level of mediocrity around us and the level everybody else is working on. We want to rise above it, cut through it, be unique, and accomplish what we need to accomplish for ourselves.

I remember an incident in college when my father had blessed me with a new car, a 1976 Chevrolet Monte Carlo. At the time it cost fifty-six hundred dollars, which would be the equivalent today of thirty thousand dollars. It was very cold and snowy up in Syracuse in the northeast of New York state, and unfortunately, I was partying a little too much in my college days as well. I cracked up the car a few times.

I remember having to go to him one particular time, not the first time, and needing fifteen hundred dollars to repair the car. Very embarrassed, tail between my legs, I felt ashamed that I had screwed up yet again. I went to him and asked him for the money. He gave it to me, but I could see the disappointment and frustration in his eyes. I remember thinking that was the reason I wanted money. Because if I screwed up again I never wanted to have to tell anybody. I wanted to be able to fix it myself.

I wished I had that fifteen hundred dollars so I didn't have to go and face Dad and experience that shame, frustration, humiliation and his disappointment. Now fortunately, I was able to rebound from that and always have had a great relationship with my father. I was able to bless him as he got older just as he blessed me through the years of my life. So that incident became a minor "aha" moment, but it was a great motivator for me at the time. It inspired me to make sure I had money to buy my way out of anything I screwed up.

So, remember, money is freedom. My father used to say that money was the lubricant for the engine of happiness. He said you could live without it, but life was a lot easier if you had it. This is true in business and in life. We want money, and we want accomplishments so we can do what we want with nobody telling us where to go or what to do.

Money gave me the freedom to explore other areas. It gave me the freedom to pursue offbeat, exciting adventures like driving in harness races and playing jai alai. Hoofbeats magazine ran a story in their May 2013 issue about me being the only person ever to compete in two pari-mutual sports as an active participant. It allowed me to write books, invest in companies, fund ministries, help charities and many other things because I had the resources and freedom to travel where I wanted, do what I wanted, invest in what I wanted, and start the businesses I wanted. Not all of them worked, but many of them did. And had I not had these resources, I would have been trapped under somebody's thumb, doing what they told me the rest of my life and feeling like I was in prison until I was finally old enough to retire or I died. Not my idea of a good plan!

TAKE⚡ACTION

• Move forward in your career as quickly as possible—but not so quickly that you miss picking up what you need for your future along the way.

• Dig down deep in your heart to discover what motivates you. Then go after it. For example, I discovered that freedom was a major motivator for me. And having money is one major ingredient for freedom. Knowing this helped me clarify my goals. What are yours?

• How do you define freedom?

CHAPTER 3

ENJOY THE RIDE

SNAPSHOT
1. Discover why having passion for your work is critical to your long-term success.

2. Learn the essential attitude necessary to get you across the finish line for ongoing success.

3. Understand why it's important to enjoy life now and how that improves the quality of your performance and success.

When I was thinking about my career path and contemplating my options, I couldn't stand the thought of a job that required constant repetition and doing the same thing every day like being a mailman or a bank teller. There's nothing wrong with those two jobs, but the thought of doing the same thing day in and day out over the course of years in a lifetime would feel like prison to me. That's my personality and the way I'm wired. Another guy may love that. He may love the security of the routine and knowing what his day will look like. To me, that's what the corporate world represented.

Regardless of which path you choose, corporate or entrepreneur, remember one thing—enjoy the ride. Don't wait until retirement to live. Your life, your work, should not be torture or a jail. It should be passion and excitement. When a ball player goes to play ball, I assume he's excited about it. When a musician gets on stage to play, I assume he's excited about it. He has passion for what he is doing and strives to be excellent at it. That doesn't mean he won't have a bad day or a bad week. Of course he will. We're all human, so we all have that. But for the most part, he loves what he's doing. You want this passion and joy.

You don't want to live all your life to work for retirement and then find out you're sick and unable to enjoy it, or you died before you could enjoy it. Of course, you want to have a happy retirement and a plan for retirement, but you need to enjoy the ride. Life was meant to be enjoyed, even with the bumps and obstacles. Work and career were meant to be enjoyed and should give you a sense of fulfillment. You need either a passion for the profession or a desire to make enough money to have freedom to do whatever you want. Ideally, you have both passion and a desire to make money, but you must have at least one.

For me, advertising was different and a lot more exciting than the typical corporate job because we were always doing new campaigns. As a matter of fact, it was like baseball. When I was growing up, I always wanted to be a baseball player. At some point I realized that dream wouldn't come true because I lived in New York and only got to play three months out of the year. Therefore, I could not compete against those kids in Arizona, California, and Florida who got to play the whole year. So I looked for the next best thing and that was advertising. Advertising had teamwork, newness, and excitement. There were campaigns to be won, clients to be won, and new stuff to do every day. It was exciting and invigorating, and for me, it was my ideal corporate profession.

We measured our success by the impact our campaigns had on our clients' brands—our wins and losses. You knew who in the industry was the best, who the champions were each year, and it changed based on accomplishment. I found that very exciting.

After NW Ayer Advertising, I worked at Bozell & Jacobs as well as Kornhauser and Calene. After several years in New York, I went to Florida and opened up my own agency, Oliver Kashmere Associates Advertising & Public Relations, as I believed I had acquired the experience and expertise necessary to run and grow my own agency. Of course it didn't hurt that now I was the boss! I was determined to call my own shots. Win, lose, or draw, I had to know that no one had deprived me of the chance to swing for success on my own terms. Then I founded Intermedia Marketing Solutions, which we started with six employees, on a borrowed hundred thousand dollars, and eventually built into a company with two hundred employees and fifteen million dollars a year in revenue.

After a very successful run, our company went public. Several years later I sold my interest in that business to begin focusing more on charity and ministry work. However, my business career continued as I got involved in real estate, publishing, food distribution, renewable energy and business and marketing consulting. I'm happy to report that today people pay me a lot of money to give them ideas, options, and strategies as well as negotiate for them and set up businesses from a strategic and operational standpoint. I still love it—dealing with different companies, developing different strategies and experiencing the payoff! Watching our work benefit others is so much fun!

As you can see, I still have the same drive I always had as a young man. I love doing new things because I find them exciting and interesting. I am also an author. I have written many books, and this is my ninth. I speak publicly on a variety of different topics, my favorite being God, and then, of course, business, marketing and advertising. I also help people struggling with drug addiction and speak extensively on that topic as well. I'll tell you more about that stuff as we go along.

The key is you want to enjoy what you do. You want to have passion and excitement for what you do in life. When I was hiring people to work at my TV production company and when I was hiring for other companies I owned or managed, I would look for two things in a person. The first will guarantee a person's success as far as I am concerned as an employer—passion for the industry.

If you have passion for what you're doing, you will succeed. There's no question in my mind. If you have passion, are reasonably intelligent and willing to learn, you will succeed. You can't buy passion for something. You can't teach it. It has to be there. If someone is passionate about something, they are worth their weight in gold. You can't even put a price on it. It is that valuable.

The other type of person who will succeed is the person who says, "I want to make a lot of money. I will do anything you tell me to do. Tell me how." That person who is totally trainable, teachable, and motivated to succeed will succeed. Because they are willing to listen to instruction, they will do it right. They don't have the attitude of not trusting the expert's opinion and wanting to do it their own way. They are so hungry for financial gain and so grateful for an opportunity to make money, they will follow instructions perfectly and do whatever you tell them. That type of person can succeed as well.

Here's another lesson from my father. He always said, "Why would you be a waiter in a bagel place where you make a four-dollar tip for serving a meal when you could be a waiter in a steak house where you make a forty-dollar tip for serving a meal? It's the exact same work but you get paid ten times the money." Obviously the only difference is the price of the steak meal is much greater than the price of a bagel meal, and people are tipping you a percentage of the cost of the meal.

My dad was always a genius like that, looking for the loophole and the angle within the system to beat it. Not saying I am a genius, but definitely wired to think that way and I know I inherited that from him. But, it makes a lot of sense. It goes back to that same theory we talked about earlier where you need to be working where the action is—as I would call it, the big leagues. Remember, you are better off being the club house boy or assistant for the Yankees than you are being vice president for a single A minor league team in upstate New York. Why? Because things are happening where the Yankees are and not much is happening in upstate New York. Your work in upstate New York won't be noticed by nearly as many people who can influence or help your future... but your work for the Yankees will be and people can improve your career.

I really wanted to get ahead in business, and the best advice I ever got came in college. At that point, one of my good friends' father, Garrett Bewkes, was the number two executive at Norton Simon under David Mahoney (who one year was the highest paid executive in America). At the time Norton Simon was one of the largest companies in the United States. So my buddy's dad was way up in the business world. He had achieved all the success I could ever dream of, and I knew he knew the secret to success. I couldn't wait to ask him what it was. I was sure there was a shortcut. I was sure he was going to tell me, and I was very excited to hear what it was going to be.

Finally, I got my chance. We were at my friend's bachelor party in Darien, Connecticut, which is where many of the wealthiest people in America live. I went up to my friend's dad and said, "Mr. Bewkes, I have a question for you. What's the secret? How did you do it? Tell me. I'm just about to graduate and I'm so excited."

He had the key to success because he had done it. He would tell me the way. I would duplicate what he had done, and I would have everything he had. It was a simple, easy plan.

However, this man looked me dead in the eye without missing a beat and he said, "There is no secret. It was hard work. I worked my butt off. You look at me now and you see the result of thirty years of hard work. I earned everything I got."

I was deflated. I thought, you must be kidding me. There's no secret? There's no shortcut? There's no formula? In reality he had just given me the formula, but it was one of hard work, not an easy shortcut.

Well, let me tell you something. That didn't stop me or deter me. Of course, I wanted there to be a shortcut. I always want there to be a shortcut. I'll always want the angle and the plan to get there quicker, but if there wasn't one, that was okay. It just meant I would have to do it the regular way, but it wasn't going to stop me from getting what I wanted. I was going to do whatever it took, and that advice was the best advice I could have gotten. I knew the path, and there wasn't a shortcut. So, if I wanted to accomplish this goal, I had to do whatever it took to get it done the long way, the hard way. I was willing to do that. Why? Because the goal was so important to me.

That's how you know you're doing something you love and are passionate about. Even if money is your goal, you're willing to do whatever it takes to get the job done. For me, when I was hired at NW Ayer Advertising as a typist, I was at the office at six in the morning even though work didn't start until nine. I couldn't wait to get there. It would be like a ball player getting called up to the Yankees and going to Yankee Stadium to play for the first time in his life. I knew I just wanted to be there. I wanted to be around the people. I wanted to learn as quickly as possible, and I was willing to do whatever it took to get the job done.

They gave us an employee handbook when we were first hired. There were eleven hundred employees in the company, and our office took up seven floors of a fifty-story building. Management was on the forty-first floor, and my job on the AT&T account was on the fortieth floor.

I hung up the photos of the top dozen management guys in the company in my bedroom and stared at their faces every night. Why do you think I did that? Because I wanted to recognize them in the elevators and the halls. I wanted to be able to call them by name and introduce myself. These guys could help advance my career. They could change my life overnight. So, I didn't wait accidentally to figure out who they were. I studied who they were and looked for my opportunity. I seized it when it came.

Let me give you this example I give to young entrepreneurs, marketing people, and people looking to get into the job market. If while you're reading this book, your mother who lived out of state was critically ill and dying—and I hope you haven't experienced this—what would you do if you got that call? I would assume your plan would be to put the book down, race to the airport, and get on the next plane to be with her so you could say goodbye. I assume if there were traffic along the way as you pulled up into the airport, you wouldn't even park your car. You would actually leave it right in front of the terminal door. Why? Normally that's crazy. You would never do that. What if they towed your car? What if someone stole it? What if something else happened? No, but you have to get on that plane. You have to see your dying mother. It's not negotiable. It has to happen. So you're going to do things you normally wouldn't do.

You race into the terminal to the ticket counter, and you see a hundred people in line in front of you. Now what are you going to do? Are you going to turn around and say, "Okay, I can't see my dying mother. I've missed the opportunity to do the thing that is most important to me right now in my life. I'm going home. I've failed"? No, of course not!

I assume you would do one of two things. Either you would run to the front of the line screaming, "Hey, I have an emergency. Sorry to cut you off, but this is an emergency." Or you would one by one talk to the people in front of you and say, "Please, you've got to let me in front of you. My mother's dying, I've got to get to New York."

Either way you're going to get to the front of that line. Why? Because you have to. It's critical. It means everything. So you're going to do whatever it takes to get that job done. That's the attitude I had in business and that's the attitude you have to have in business. You have to do whatever it takes to get the job done. You have to go above and beyond.

TAKE ACTION

- Don't wait until retirement to enjoy your life. Some people never make it! Rather, enjoy your life, and your work, as you go.

- Finding work that suits you—that you can be passionate about—is crucial for enjoying the ride. If you love action, you don't want to be stuck in a predictable job. And if you love security and consistency, you don't want to get a job where what is required of you and what you do changes constantly.

- Are you passionate about your current work? If not, what action can you take today to move at least one step closer to more fulfilling work?

- You need to have either a passion for what you do or make enough money at it to make it worth it for you. The money is only good insofar as it helps you achieve the goals that motivate you. You have to know what those are!

- Be proactive. Don't wait for opportunity to come to you. Go after it! Going all-in and doing whatever it takes will put you ahead of the competition.

- Do you currently have the "do whatever it takes" attitude necessary for long-term, sustainable success? If not, think more on your motivation to succeed. Is it a big enough motivation?

CHAPTER 4

WORK SMART

SNAPSHOT

1. Learn the importance of going the extra mile.

2. Discover why you should always treat everyone with dignity and respect.

3. Understand the value of consistently striving for excellence in your work.

I previously told you I was at the office at six in the morning every morning when I was hired on as a typist at NW Ayer Advertising, but that wasn't all I did. I volunteered to help on other projects in other departments, but only after I had completed all my work at a high level of excellence.

That set me apart from others. I said, "Is there any other work I can do? Can I stay late and help you guys with something else?" I wanted to be around the movers and shakers of the company. I volunteered to be part of charity drives the executives were participating in so I could get to know them better and quicker and show them I was a go-getter. I was willing to do whatever it took to get the job done. I wanted to prove they could count on me. That strategy paid off handsomely and in spades for my career in advertising and in many other business endeavors.

Also, you need to make sure you don't align yourself with any cliques in the corporate world. Why? Because you don't know who knows who. You don't know if the secretary is the boss's niece, daughter, sister-in-law or cousin. You just don't know. You're working in a company with a lot of people, and you need everybody to like you and think you're amazing. They don't all have to be your best friends, but you don't want to have any enemies. So, in that regard, you work hard for everybody—no matter who your boss is, whether you like them or not, or whether you agree with their strategy, instructions or management style.

I had a split job in advertising when I was promoted out of being a typist after three months at the company. I went to work as an assistant account executive, and I worked half the time for an account management supervisor on AT&T and the other half of the time for a lady who supervised client billing.

I did not like the billing lady very much. She was mean, cold, didn't care about me, and wasn't well-liked within the company. But she had been there for many years. She had a position of power and she was a crappy boss. That's the nicest way I can say it.

On the other side, the account management boss was amazing. He was inspiring, encouraging, taught me, molded me, shaped me, and it was a great learning experience. But I worked just as hard for the billing lady and didn't complain. I didn't say anything, even though I knew there was no reward in it. I knew other people were watching, and I didn't comment about her behind her back. I didn't say negative things, and I did my job. I did the same thing throughout my career.

When I got a promotion to the traffic department (the department in the agency that coordinates all the creative and production work and is responsible for all insertion deadlines for magazine, television, radio and print ads), I worked very hard in that department. Six other people were in that department and saw how hard I was working. When some of them got promoted later, they each wanted me on their team.

That's what happens. People are watching you. People are watching what you're doing all of the time. Now, when you go home from work and are hanging out with your friends who don't work in your industry, you can do whatever you want. But at the office, you don't want to develop a clique of friends that separates you from the rest of the company. You just want to be known for your hard work and your effort. You want to be dependable and reliable. You want to be the guy who gets the job done, the go-to guy people can count on to do the right thing. They can count on your trust, your confidentiality, and that you're going to do what it takes to get the job done.

When people from your company get promoted or get recruited by other companies, who are they going to want on their team? The guy who was their buddy, who was slacking off, who was drinking with them, who was cursing with them, telling jokes, screwing the company, stealing supplies? Is that the guy they want working for them or with them? Or will they prefer the guy they saw busting his butt to do whatever it took to get the job done, the guy who strove for excellence? Of course they're going to want the guy they can trust who strives for excellence, especially when their job is dependent on it and when they're in control. Wouldn't you? It won't be about friendship anymore. The last person I want to hire is my slack-off friend. I want the guy who is going to get the job done and make me look good.

That's the guy you need to be, period. You need to be the guy who gets ahead. That guy succeeds by being single-focused and determined. You can do that when you're young, when you don't have family or other responsibilities. You can be single-focused on getting ahead, like I did in high school, college and then professionally. Whatever it took to get ahead in school, to get out of there early because I didn't want to be there anymore. I wanted to get started with my life. Did it pay off? Oh man, did it pay off.

One day, I was sitting in my office at NW Ayer Advertising at 6:30 in the morning, I was the only one there, when the number three guy in charge of the company, Dom Rossi, came down to my floor looking for something. I said, "Can I help you, Dom?" Because, of course, I recognized him from his picture I had hanging in my room at home.

He said, "Yeah, I'm looking for Peter Nathan, an account executive. I need something for our business pitch with AT&T today." The AT&T account, which our company had for many years, was up for review. AT&T was splitting up the company due to a federally mandated deregulation, and we were competing against Oglivy and Mather, Doyle Dane Bernbach, and some of the larger ad agencies in the world.

The competition was down to four final agencies. We were one of them, fighting for our lives to keep the account. It was worth five hundred million dollars per year in billing.

This was the day our executives, Lou Hagopian, George Eversman, Jerry Ciano and Dom Rossi where going out by limo to AT&T headquarters in Bedminster, New Jersey, to make the pitch to save the account.

Dom had asked for Peter Nathan. I said, "Dom, he's not in yet, but can I help you with anything?" He said he was looking for a specific document, and I was able to get him to the document he needed. He looked at me and said, "Hey, why don't you come with us today." I was shocked. He said, "Yeah, come with us. We're making the pitch to AT&T."

So, there I was, now at 7:30 in the morning, on the way in the limo to the most important business pitch of this agency's history, sitting with the four top executives of the company. That day changed my life. That moment in time changed my life. My career skyrocketed. Dom Rossi took a personal liking to me, and he advanced me through the agency ranks. I became a fast track executive in that company.

Now, let me tell you something. I'm glad it happened that day. I obviously can't guarantee that if you're in the office 6:30 every morning the same thing will happen to you, but I want to share the most important concept I can tell you. I would have gotten that advancement in my career one way or the other. It was going to happen. It may have taken me longer. I might have done it the hard way, but that was my goal. I wanted it and I was going to get it. I was a determined man, and nothing was going to stop me from getting to that goal. Nothing should stop you from getting yours either. I had a single focus. That was my determination, and I was going to make it happen.

My career leapfrogged five years ahead because of that moment in time. Remember, I was willing to do what it took. I didn't know when it would happen. I just knew it would happen if I kept doing the right things.

By the way, when I went to NW Ayer Advertising from Syracuse University, they had a management training program. They wouldn't let me in it because you had to be hired out of grad school into the management training program to get in. Well, I wasn't coming from grad school but I noticed the guys in the management training program had the same ambition I did and they were on the fast track in the company.

I went to upper management and said, "Look, please let me into this management training program. I'm doing well in the company. I would benefit from it. It would help me." They said no because "rules were rules." Suffice to say I wasn't happy with their response.

I remember going to one of the senior executives at the company Tom Maxey, who headed up the AT&T account (one of the accounts I worked on). Tom was an extremely corporate guy in appearance and speech and very high up on the account management side, and he gave me words of wisdom that stayed with me throughout my career. He said the best lesson he ever had learned in business was "the squeaky wheel gets the oil." He encouraged me to keep trying to get the agency to allow me to be part of the management training program. That was a great bit of advice and a great lesson I used often in my career—as valid and relevant today as it ever was.

With that in mind, I formed my own informal "club" in the agency called ADClub. Once a week, after work, I would meet with a couple of other young executives who weren't in the management training program but who wanted extra training. I organized this with my buddy, Andy Brief, and we invited a speaker from a different department in our company each week. We had a guy from marketing, from media, and from production. One week we had a new business account pitched to us exactly as it had been done that morning for a potential client, and ADClub really started to grow within the agency.

The agency's in-house newsletter wrote about us, and we started to invite outside speakers. We got Whit Hobbs, who was a legendary advertising writer at the time and wrote for Adweek, to come and speak to us. It didn't hurt that we did our research and found out that Whit was an avid swimmer. Next to advertising this was his passion. So when we invited him to speak, we had a messenger hand deliver a pair of personalized swimming trunks that had the ADClub logo on them.

Whit loved that and agreed to speak. After all we were advertising men, out-of-the-box thinkers. Would you expect anything less? Whit came in and delivered a great speech. He was inspiring. Then a couple of weeks later he called and said he was writing an article about us. He wrote the article about ADClub in Adweek magazine.

After that we invited Lou Hagopian, the chairman of NW Ayer Advertising, to speak to the group. We had to for political reasons. Hey, we weren't idiots! Soon after, in the next month's issue of Advertising Age magazine, the industry bible, pictures of Lou and me with some of the ADClub gang appeared for the whole world to see. (Justice. Baby, justice!) Getting exposure for the agency in two of the largest industry magazines was a very favorable thing. Of course, it didn't hurt that we were the focus of the exposure!

As a result of that, management came back to me and said they were going to change the rules and let me in the management training program. From that point on, if they saw someone deserving to be in the program, they asked the person to join, regardless of what college they came from. Graduate school was no longer a mandatory requirement for the management training program at NW Ayer Advertising. That was amazing. We changed history because we weren't willing to settle.

There are only two options when you come to an obstacle. You knock it down, or you go around it. That's the attitude you have to have. Either way, it is not going to stop you. Some obstacles you have to figure out. Some may take longer to go around, but figuring it out is how you get ahead. That type of determination and enthusiasm can take you a long way. One way or the other, you get your goal. You accomplish it.

For example, I had an incident with a guy when I worked at NW Ayer Advertising. He was an older, senior guy who didn't like me very much at all. I don't know why. I didn't have much contact with the guy, but I assumed it was because I was a rising executive and he was an older guy on the way down. He just did not like me. He made it clear he didn't like me, though we didn't have much interaction.

So, one day I decided to write him a letter. Basically, I won him over in the letter. I said I didn't understand why he didn't like me because I hadn't done anything to him or wronged him in any way. Quite the opposite, I respected him very much and wanted to be able to learn from him, his experience, and expertise. After he received the letter, he was kind to me and wonderful. It changed his heart and attitude.

It's not always about writing a letter, but it is always about communicating! I don't care how you do it—in writing, verbally, with action—but you had better be able to communicate with people, reach them and touch them on many levels (mind, heart and soul) if you want to be successful. Remember, these are tools in your work belt, but you need them all.

An obstacle was in my way. I didn't need an enemy in the agency, and I won him over. That's what I mean about being focused and willing to do whatever it takes to get the job done. I'm sure no one had ever treated him that way before. He was a crusty guy, certainly not a warm, loving, kind guy. Nonetheless, I did what it took to win him over. I'm not saying you should write every person a letter. I'm saying you do what it takes. You treat each situation individually, but you do what it takes to get the job done.

On that note let me tell you a story. Many years later as an entrepreneur, I was working on our 70 MW solar project. We named it "HERO" Solar, a great marketing name for the project, which got us a ton of free press and positive PR. It was an acronym for Hamilton Energy Resource Opportunities LLC, I named the company that purposely so it would be known as the HERO project. Later on in the project's development First Solar (one of the largest and best solar companies in the world) came in and partnered with us. As such we were exposed to their technical team and worked with them very closely.

I had just taken in a minority partner into the project. His name was Mohammed Alrai, from RAI Energy. So we had me, born Jewish and now a born again Christian, Mohammed Alrai, and the First Solar team, which consisted of people named Enrique Silva, Ravi Beeravalli, Omar Aboudaher, Vladimir Chadliev, Justin Walters and a brilliant woman named Assawari Pawar.

I was amazed at the wide variety of cultural and religious backgrounds of the people who worked on this project, but more importantly I was blown away and never forgot the impression that I captured in my heart and mind when I saw these brilliant people from different backgrounds and religions all focused solely and with great diligence on the task at hand.

The solar project featured their ingenuity, creativity, knowledge, wisdom and experience merging together for one purpose—to move the project forward. Working like a well-oiled machine, we brought about the forward movement and successful completion of the assignment. It was awe-inspiring. I thought, Wow this is what heaven must be like when we're all together worshiping and focused on God with no distraction and experiencing great joy in what we are doing. Our differences won't matter.

This is a great reminder and proof of the benefits and importance of focusing on the task at hand. Nobody in that group allowed any of their backgrounds, prejudices, thoughts, influences or anything else going on in their lives (including personal issues, health issues or problems) to affect their performance on the project. They were single-focused on the task at hand. How beautiful and brilliant it was.

TAKE ACTION

• Don't play office politics. It's a form of short cutting that will make you enemies in the long run—and you never know who you'll have to work with (or for) later! Instead, move forward by being the hardest-working, easiest-to-work-with person in the place.

• Being a hard, reliable, efficient worker will get you farther in the long run than cultivating "buddies." Remember, when jobs are on the line, people will hire and promote those who will make them look best by getting the work done, rather than pals who slack off.

• What can you do to separate yourself from others and stand out?

• I jumped ahead five years in advertising because I was in the office putting in work when nobody else was. Good breaks are good breaks, but you'll put yourself in the best position for good breaks by being there and working hard.

• In business, "the squeaky wheel gets the oil." Don't be rude or abrasive, but do push against barriers. You can either knock down obstacles or find a way to go around them, but the one thing you cannot do is let them stop you! Figure out how to neutralize or overcome the barrier, and don't take "no" for an answer.

• Go the extra mile to accomplish your work in excellence to consistently make a positive impact.

CHAPTER 5

DIFFERENTIATE YOURSELF

SNAPSHOT

1. Learn the importance of knowing where you want to go and what it takes to get there.

2. Understand how necessary skills, abilities, training and experience work together catapulting you to greatness in your industry.

3. Discover how your uniqueness will put you over the top to success and the value of developing and maintaining a reputation of integrity for your success.

In this day and age of internet, computers, and technology, still remember this—nothing replaces personal touch and personal communication. What do I mean? Let me tell you a story. I was looking for work. I was out of a job, and I was specifically looking for work in the advertising industry where my degree was.

At this point in time I had left New York and moved to Florida, and I went to work as the advertising director of a large stock brokerage firm. Working there I realized I didn't want to be on the client side but wanted back into the agency side, so I went looking for another position. However, the economy was slow for a couple of months, and I got a little discouraged. I called my father who said he had noticed an ad in the Wall Street Journal. A TV production company in south Florida was looking for a marketing manager. I was a little discouraged at that point, not very motivated, and my father said, "Look, you should go down there in person and drop your resume off. You never know who knows who or what might happen. You can go in, a guy can see you, he can like you and hire you on the spot."

See, my dad knew the value of one-to-one contact. He knew the value of going to a place yourself. So, I did that. I went down to the place to hand my resume off to the secretary, had a little conversation with her, and later that day got a call back from the owner to have an interview. I went in and interviewed for the job. He had a stack of resumes on his desk and he said, "Let me ask you a question. Why should I hire you? I've got the best talent in the world looking for this job."

I said to him, "Listen, you have all those resumes on your desk. Here's my suggestion. Hire me, and give me a month. If I'm not your guy, you can always go back and hire one of those other guys. You already have their information and resumes, but I am your guy. I'm here now. I'm ready to go, and I'm going to get the job done. Just give me a chance." He said yes.

That was the beginning of an illustrious run in television production. I worked for that company for a couple of years and then started my own TV production company. We started with six employees, on a borrowed hundred thousand dollars, and over the years built it up to over two hundred employees doing $15 million a year in revenue. We went public, I sold the company, and my life was awesome. Here's the point, if I had just sent in my resume, I would never have gotten that job. It would have been in that pile, and my qualifications wouldn't have gotten me the job.

However, because I went down there personally the secretary took a liking to me, and she told the boss to interview me. He listened to his secretary. So, here is the highest paid man in the company, the owner, listening to the secretary. Why? Because he values and respects her opinion. He works with her every day and trusts her, so she has a lot of influence on him.

I've been in other situations where I've walked into offices to hand in resumes or to make contacts early in the morning, and the owner was the only one there. The secretary hadn't come in yet, and the owner was there. What a great way to meet the owner of a business and get to talk to him privately. I'm not saying that in every case you'll be able to go personally and drop off a resume or set up a meeting that way, but you need to look for those personal opportunities.

We're talking about doing stuff that sets you apart from everybody else, separating yourself from the crowd.

We need to be unique. Advertising taught me that. When I was at Kornhauser and Calene advertising, we came up with a campaign for Arm & Hammer baking soda. The campaign was to take the product and flush it down the toilet because your toilet smelled. Also, you needed to put it in your car because your car smelled. So, we had taken this product that was only previously used for refrigerators and baking and created new markets for it.

We actually got people to buy the product and flush it down the toilet. You know how brilliant that was! It was genius. It was out of the box, strategic thinking to increase market share, come up with new applications, and invent new ways to do business. You need to do that in life and business, not just advertising.

I have a buddy who lives in New York, and he said, "Oh, I'm really depressed. There are no jobs in New York. I'm not getting a job, and it's very frustrating." I told him I guaranteed I could get him a job.

I told him all he needed to do was to go out in a three-piece suit and put a sandwich board around him that said, I'm looking for work. Here are my qualifications. I'm hard-working, a fast learner, and do whatever it takes to get the job done. Somebody walking down the street on Sixth Avenue in New York City will hire you. You will get a job. You go out there for a couple of days, and you will have a job, probably in the first or second day.

He didn't want to do that. So, I guess he didn't want the job badly enough because every once in a while in the New York Post you would see an article where an unemployed executive did that. He went out, stood out on the street in a suit with a sandwich board advertising himself. Who wouldn't want that guy. If I was an employer, I would want that guy—the guy who had enough guts and courage to go out and stand on the street corner and advertise himself. He set himself apart from the crowd. He was willing to do whatever it took, and he got hired.

My buddy was claiming he was so desperate for a job and would do anything, but that wasn't true. He might have been desperate for work, but he wasn't willing to do whatever it took. He wasn't willing to stand on the street corner for one or two days to get a job. He had plenty of time, months, to sit around and complain about not getting a job when the bottom line was he wasn't willing to do what it took. I have no respect for that. Remember, you make your own breaks.

Ray Negron, who was an executive for the Yankees, worked his way up from scratch. He was a kid off the street, literally. One day he was hanging out with friends outside of Yankee Stadium, and George Steinbrenner, then the owner of the Yankees, took a liking to him and wanted to give him a break. He hired him as an intern and groomed him, and Ray Negron worked his way up in the organization into a management position with the New York Yankees. Why? Because somebody gave him an opportunity, and he took advantage of it.

The question is, how badly do you want it, and what are you willing to do about it? So, remember, when someone tries to mentor you in your life and in business, they want you to succeed. They will train you and grow you and give you guidance as you go. You want to take advantage of those who have been down the road because they can tell you what it's like. They can help you navigate the trail and get you where you're going.

A young man named Josh once asked me for advice about going into advertising. Josh did everything I told him to do—taking the right college classes, interviewing with companies, taking first and second jobs that would build his resume and gather him the expertise necessary to succeed long term, asking for raises, getting ahead in the company, having mentors, separating himself from the crowd and demonstrating excellence. He followed my instructions, step by step, and he wanted it. I recognized he had the same desire to get ahead as I did, and in five years he was a top ad executive, making a top salary because he knew where he wanted to go and he was willing to do whatever it took to get the job done.

What do you do if you are a baseball player and you can't hit a curve ball? Do you quit and give up? No, of course not. That's absurd. You practice hitting curve balls. Do you just have to practice an hour a day? I don't know how long you have to practice. Only you know how long you have to practice. You have to practice as long as it takes until you can hit curve balls. One guy may have to practice ten minutes while another guy has to practice an hour a day the rest of his life. It doesn't matter. You're responsible for doing what you need to do to get to that level where you need to compete—at least at a minimum level. If you don't do that, you don't play on the team, you don't make it, you're out.

It's the same in business. You must do whatever it takes to get yourself to at least the minimum level you need to compete, though obviously you should be striving for a maximum level. There was a guy in advertising named Cliff Freeman. He was starting his own agency and was pitching the Nike account at the time. He was a one-man agency going up against these major agencies like Oglivy and Mather with over a thousand employees, so he was clearly out matched, out-manned, and outnumbered. But he was very smart and went into the Nike pitch by himself, but he wasn't alone.

You see, he placed eleven cardboard cutouts of himself in the conference chairs representing his team. Nike bought it! They loved his creativity, daring and boldness and gave him the account, and it launched his agency into the stratosphere. He was smart and thought outside the box. He wasn't like everybody else. That's what you have to do.

When I was a rookie at NW Ayer Advertising, I used to send memos to the management guys. I used to tell them things I observed in the company, which I thought were intelligent comments. In the summers, when they gave us Friday afternoons off, I thanked them. I told them I felt we got just as much done in the half day as we would have during a whole day because everybody was so appreciative of them giving us the afternoon off. Also, if I saw a way the company could improve, I sent these guys a memo. That was before they even knew who I was.

One day, one of highest ranking management guys in the agency, George Eversman (Executive Vice President), was talking to his friend, Garrett Bewkes (my friend's dad

I told you about earlier) at a cocktail party in Connecticut as they lived in the same town. Bewkes mentioned he knew me and George said, "Yeah, I get more memos from that kid Levine than from my management team." He said that in a complimentary way. Here I had the top guys in one of the biggest agencies in the world, who knew me and were watching my work. That's what you want to happen.

When I owned and managed my TV production company, we had two hundred employees and they all had ideas about how to make the company better. I really truly wanted to hear them, but I couldn't always act on or implement every idea they came up with. Why? Well, their timing may have been wrong. Maybe there was something going on that I couldn't share with that employee at that particular time so, while I liked the idea, I couldn't implement it then. There may have been other reasons that it didn't make sense, but if you were the owner of the company, would you want your employees to stop telling you their ideas? No, of course not. I would never want that.

Just remember that when you share input with management or bosses and they don't love every idea you say or they don't implement every idea you have, that's okay. You keep coming back with the next one. You don't take it personally. You're not offended by that because there could be many variables you are not aware of. Do not stop sharing ways to better the company or the product regardless of whether your last idea was liked or not.

I would always want my employees and friends to tell me the truth, whether I implemented their last idea or not, or liked it or not. Your bosses want the same from you.

By the way, while we're at it, just a side note about social media. Don't be an idiot and blow up your career by posting something stupid on social media. Right now, it's Facebook, Twitter, Snapchat, Instagram, LinkedIn. In the years to come, those names may be obsolete, and there will be twenty other ways to communicate, but the bottom line is the same.

Remember what I told you. When I left my apartment to go to work, whether I was walking down the street, on the train, or at the office, I assumed I was on stage in a Broadway play. I was in character. I was in role, and I didn't let my guard down until I came back home that night and shut my apartment door. Then, I could do whatever I wanted to do. But while I was out there, I was playing that role of executive, striving to be the best and never letting my guard down. So don't be an idiot. Don't post about partying, bongs, bombs, guns, sex, politics and religion on social media or in any other public forums.

You can have an opinion. You can share it with your best friend. You can do anything you want, but not in the context of the office or your professional career. You can't do these things publicly. They will destroy you. There will be silent prejudices against you, and you don't want that to happen. You want to be the guy everybody looks at and says, "I wish I had that guy working for me. Look how hard that man works. Wow, that guy is amazing."

There will be very few like you because most people will sink to a level of mediocrity around them. Most people would rather not work, screw off, hang out and do nothing as opposed to getting work done. You need to be the other guy—the one who doesn't stop, who keeps going, who gets it done. That's who you are.

At the end of the day, you both will be at the office at the same time. You both will go to work for a lot of your adult life, but I have this very simple theory. If I could do two years of work in one year's time and take a year off, I would want to do that. If I could do six years of work in three years' time and have three years off, I would want to do that. I wouldn't want to space it out and say, let me work easy over the six years and not strain myself. No, I would rather kill myself for three years and take three years off, because to me, time is so valuable.

I always wanted to get ahead quicker because it gave me options and freedom in life to do what I wanted. That's why you should want to get ahead too. Not only will you make money and have the prestige that comes with success, but it will give you options and freedom. Remember how I told you money gives you freedom? Well, time is freedom also. When you get to spend it and do with it what you want the way you choose, you will be a happy person.

I always wanted to be in the position in life where I was working because I wanted to and not because I had to. That's where you want to get too. There is no greater freedom than that, and I want you to have it. I hope this book will help you get there.

GUARD YOUR INTEGRITY

Don't ever steal anything from the company, not even a pencil. Even if you know no one is looking, or you think you'll never get caught, don't do it. It's not worth it. It's too much risk. You'll blow everything you have worked for, even if nobody catches you. If somebody sees you or suspects you, the perception of you will change dramatically. It may be tempting from time to time to take something, but I assure you it's not worth the risk. Do not do that in any circumstance. You need to be above reproach in that company, and it will come back to you in spades over time. You cannot put a price on your reputation and your integrity. They are invaluable.

Even if nobody says anything, or you don't get caught, you do not want to get labeled in somebody's mind as a thief or as not loyal. Remember, these people will be at other companies later. They will be promoted later, will possibly have the opportunity to hire you to advance your career. Whether you like them or not is irrelevant. You want to impress them with your work ethic, and you want everybody to want you to be a part of their team and their company. That is how you get ahead.

TAKE ACTION

- Strive for personal communication. It stands out more than ever in an internet world. This is true whether you're seeking a job, a promotion, or simply doing your work well.

- One human being, face to face, always has the advantage over a stack of papers on a desk, or a conglomeration of pixels on a computer screen. So go talk to people.

- How are you leaving a lasting impression on people? Most times, if you are working for others, important decisions about your career and future are made when you are not in the room.

- Look for ways to separate yourself from the rest of the crowd. Be creative and look to make your own breaks rather than waiting for them to come. Remember Cliff Freeman? He won the Nike account as a one-man advertising agency by being creative and daring.

- Take personal responsibility to do whatever it takes to develop your skills and abilities through education and hands-on training, developing relationships and other experiences to succeed in your industry.

- Give thoughtful and regular input to your higher-ups. They may not implement every idea you have, but it will put you on their radar.

• Don't put stupid things on social media. That is not the way you want to stand out. If you have questionable photos and posts on social media, you may not be able to permanently erase them—the internet remembers everything—but at least start by deleting them immediately.

• Be a person of integrity. It will make you stand out in a world without ethics—and you'll be the first chosen when they need to promote someone they trust.

CHAPTER 6

UNDERSTAND THE FUTURE VALUE OF EXPERIENCE

SNAPSHOT

1. Understand the future value of current training and on-the-job experience.

2. Discover how perception affects promotion and money matters.

3. Learn why you need to be responsible for and complete with excellence all your assignments and tasks, even the ones you don't like!

Remember this as you go because it's a negotiating issue down the line. When you're training with a company and they are teaching you something, the next company is going to pay you for what this company trained you to do. The current company nine times out of ten will not.

This was another lesson I learned from my father that was true. It's a known business fact. If a company hires you at twelve bucks an hour and trains you for a year or two, that company is going to have a problem paying you thirty dollars an hour. Why? Not that you may not be worth thirty dollars an hour after a year or two of training, but they hired you at twelve. So, they will always see you as a twelve-dollar-an-hour guy. You might get raised to fifteen or eighteen from them, but you're not going to thirty.

The same thing goes for annual salary. If they hired you at fifty thousand dollars a year, they are going to have a problem paying you two hundred thousand. They won't have a problem paying you seventy or eighty thousand as you progress, but they will have a problem paying you two or three hundred thousand. However, the next company (or boss) won't.

Why? Because the next company isn't seeing you as the person they hired and trained. They are seeing you as having performed those duties at the other company, and they are willing to pay you the true value of what you're worth. The bottom line is in most cases you'll never get paid what you're worth by the first company (or boss) who hires you. So, you're not going to stay at that job.

With that said, it doesn't mean you don't give your best and your utmost at all times. You always do for anybody. My dad always said, if you're going to work for a guy and take his money, he deserves your best. And I believe that same thing. If I'm not going to give you my best, I shouldn't work for you. I may not like what you're paying me. I might not agree with it, but if I agree to work for you, I owe you my best. You are going to get my best, no matter if I think I'm being paid fairly or not. You're going to do your best at all times. Otherwise, you shouldn't work for that company (or boss).

Understand this. The way to make more money in the corporate world is to sell the experience you have learned from the last company to the next company along the way. Of course, there are some factors in that. If you have stock incentives in a company, it may not be worth jumping for an extra thirty thousand dollars or even a hundred thousand dollars to the next company. But that's an individual decision. For the most part, the next company will always pay you more for the experience you obtained at the other company.

It's not unusual to see an executive changing companies to advance their career. I'm not talking about every year or two, but to make a few career moves to get paid more money is understandable or even expected. Of course, you're going to first ask the guys who trained you for more money—and sometimes when there is a management change, you'll be able to get that—but usually that's not the way it works. Just remember that you want to get as much training as possible, as quickly as possible, so that your worth increases in the marketplace more and more and as fast as possible.

The quicker you get the training, the quicker you get more responsibility and are able to function at a high level of proficiency, the quicker your value and worth increases and the quicker you get the promotions.

IT'S YOUR RESPONSIBILITY WHETHER YOU LIKE IT OR NOT

When you work for someone, it's your responsibility to get the job done. I remember one particularly disturbing incident in my career early on. I was an account executive at Kornhauser and Calene, and a new outside account supervisor was just hired into the agency. His name was Jerry Bond. He was very straight-laced with no sense of humor—the complete plastic man as I would think of him. He spoke in a monotone with very little personality.

That's not to say he wasn't a nice guy. I'm sure he was, but suffice to say he was not one of the boys! He was very buttoned-down and corporate. I was assigned to work under him on one particular account and we had a brochure coming off the press for this particular client. In those days before computer printing, in order to make sure that the colors on the printed job would look like the artwork you submitted, you actually went down to the press and saw the first sheets come off the press. These were called press proofs.

I was playing on the company softball team with the owner's sons, a lot of the top management guys, and other friends in the agency. We had a great time at softball. It was an advertising league, so we played against other top ad agencies, two games a week during the summer. After the games it was a team ritual to all go to a nearby pub in New York City and celebrate the game, life, justice and the American way... smile!

It was a great time. I was a very good softball player and a revered member of the team. I loved to play and I didn't mind looking good doing it. The social aspect of it was amazing as well.

So, when Jerry Bond told me the morning of a game I needed to go down to a printer and look at a press proof at 5:30 p.m. I told him of course I couldn't make it. We had a softball game that night that started at 6. He looked at me sternly (and like I was crazy) and said, "I don't care. You need to be at the printer. It's your responsibility."

Despite my pleading, cajoling, and trying to wiggle out of it with every technicality I could think of, Jerry Bond was adamant that it was my responsibility. He insisted, I needed to be there and would be there or there would be serious ramifications. I told him it was pointless for me to be there, a complete waste of time, that nothing would go wrong. We had worked with these printers before and they knew what they were doing. Under protest and very upset, I reluctantly went to the printer at 5:30 p.m. knowing I would miss the 6 p.m. game. I was so mad at Jerry Bond and couldn't wait for his quick professional demise. I would show him... the nerve of him. How dare he send me to such a menial task when something so important—the softball game—needed to be played.

Well, here's how the story ends. I went down to the printer at 5:30, and wouldn't you know it. There was a mistake on the job that I caught. Had I not been there, the job would've been printed wrong. Our agency would have been liable not only for reprints but we would've missed the client deadline as they needed these brochures for a trade show the next day. So the bottom line is Bond was right and I was wrong. Lesson learned.

Although I never gave him the satisfaction of admitting he was right until now, I did learn the lesson that I need to be responsible for the things that were my responsibility, whether I liked it or not. In this instance even though I considered it a menial, trivial task, it was critical to the finished product, and I was wrong to put my own personal desires ahead of my responsibilities as an account executive.

Once I learned that lesson I never forgot it. Of course later in life I was playing the role of Jerry Bond (the drill sergeant) with young executives teaching them the importance of responsibility and follow-through. You need to learn the same in any company, business, industry, or anything you do in life. It is a critical key to success. Learn it now. Commit to excellence in this area at all costs. It will help you tremendously!

TAKE ACTION

• Things you are learning at your current company will likely make you money at your next company. Take the experience now and give the job everything, knowing the payoff will come in the next opportunity.

• Usually you will have to change companies to realize the full market value of skills you have acquired in your current job.

• Do you think you are worth more in the competitive marketplace than you are being paid now? When was the last time you asked for a raise? (Remember, the worst they could do is say no!)

• Gain as much training and skill in your current job as possible—and as quickly as possible, which will greatly increase your value in the marketplace.

• Be accountable for the things for which you'll be held responsible and do everything with excellence. Your work will be better and more reliable. You'll save yourself ulcers, and you'll stand out in most work environments, where buck-passing and blame-shifting is the norm.

CHAPTER 7

MAKE IT HAPPEN

> **SNAPSHOT**
>
> 1. Learn the critical importance of taking immediate action.
>
> 2. Discover the indispensable value of a mentor and industry relationships.
>
> 3. Understand the importance of investing now to develop future leaders.

I had a great boss named Stan Turk at Kornhauser and Calene Advertising, and he called me into his office one day. I had written what I thought was a great memo about something that had happened in the company. He called me into his office and ripped up the memo in front of me. He said, "Sit down. There are two types of people in advertising—people who stand around and just write about things that happen and people who make things happen. You're going to be one of those guys who make things happen."

That was a great lesson from Stan. He was a wonderful mentor and a great guy. He invested time in me. I watched him handle his clients and people in the company. He was honest and happy. He knew careers were built on who you knew and networking (and of course delivering quality work), and he relished those relationships with his clients. He had a wonderful career, but I will never forget that day.

The guy writing the memos is expendable and dispensable. Anybody can be that guy. That guy will not be a huge success. He wanted me to be the guy who gets things done. That man is valuable. He is irreplaceable.

Stan also taught me another great lesson. He took me to Chicago one day for a trade show with one of our clients. I had never been to Chicago, so I was excited. I was still a young advertising executive, and I was excited to be with Stan on the trip. At the trade show I was filling up bags with information from the booths, figuring the information was of extreme value. I was lugging these bags back on the plane walking down the aisle to my seat and one of the bags broke. Very embarrassed, I cleaned up all the pamphlets and brochures on the aisle and put the stuff in my suitcase.

Stan called me into his office the next day and he said, "Listen, I didn't take you to Chicago to gather pamphlets and brochures. I could have hired a minimum wage temp in Chicago for the day to do that. I took you down there to meet people and understand how things work, how agency business gets done. I wanted you to experience the relationship we have with our clients."

There was Stan again, like a father—coaching me and educating me. He wasn't upset with me. He could have stopped me the first time I picked a brochure up and told me, but he wanted me to learn. He wanted me to experience it, but he was telling me and showing me the way. I learned quickly from Stan and others like him. That's what you want to do—learn and learn quickly.

Over twenty years later, for some reason Stan was on my mind and in my heart, even though I had not seen or spoken to him since I left New York to go the promised land of Florida two decades prior. I had become a tremendous success at that point. I had started my own TV production company. I was married and had kids. I was a tremendous success by the world's standards, even by my own. I had everything I wanted, and I had thought about all the valuable lessons I learned from Stan.

He was one of a couple of bosses in particular who had invested in me and taught me those wonderful lessons. I wanted to tell him how much I appreciated that and what it meant to me, so I wrote and sent him a three-paged typed letter and basically just said thank you. I recounted some of the lessons, a couple of which I shared with you here today, he had taught me, moments that had made an impact on my life, and just let him know that it mattered. I wanted him to know I had never forgotten it, and I hoped I was making a similar impact on others, especially the lives of other young executives. I hoped I was coaching them, encouraging them, and taking a personal interest in them, as he had taken in me. I was grateful for what he did for me and thanked him.

A few weeks later, I got a letter from his daughter saying Stan had died a few weeks prior. He had died at home watching the Yankees game (Stan loved the Yankees). They came home and found him on the couch. He had died of a heart attack.

His daughter said of all the tributes they had at the funeral and all the people who spoke lovingly about Stan, none of them had the impact on their family as my letter because it was unsolicited. Of course, I didn't know Stan had already passed away when I wrote the letter. When his family saw the impact his life had on me, it didn't surprise them because they knew the kind of guy Stan was, but it served as a touching memorial for them.

I knew God had spoken to my heart at that time, and I understood why Stan was heavy on my heart and mind at just that exact time in my life. It was so I could write that letter. What a blessing. We want to be those guys too. Remember that. You want to give back and help in the same way you've been helped. That's why I'm writing this book. You need to be someone's Stan.

I want to be able to teach you, help you, encourage you, and inspire you because I know the difference an inspired life makes. I don't want you to miss that. I want you to live that—in your business, in your professional life, and in your personal life. I want you to have that at all costs. Stan had it. I have it, and I want you to have it. It's a choice you've got to make. You have to work for it. Remember what Mr. Bewkes said—no shortcuts.

TAKE ACTION

• Think about the people who have helped you. Now, look for people around you whom you can similarly help.

• Strategize ways you can go from being a talker to a doer in your workplace.

• Who are you learning from? A mentor is vital in facilitating quicker learning and application of lessons learned that will help you obtain greater success. You can also learn from others by watching them work and listening to them.

CHAPTER 8

STAY RELEVANT

SNAPSHOT

1. Learn the importance of staying relevant with trends in your industry including technology.

2. Discover how to prevent yourself from getting stuck in your career.

3. Understand why it is vital to your success to learn how to read people and recognize the appropriate time to ask for guidance.

EMBRACE TECHNOLOGY

You need to stay current on technological developments in your industry. If you're not sure if this is relevant counsel, just take a look at BlockBuster Video, Eastman Kodak, Polaroid or some other companies that died because they didn't stay ahead of the curve regarding technology.

Back in chapter 1, I told you about my friend Dave Salomone VP of one of the most well known cable television networks in the world. Dave has been a producer and editor for almost thirty years. He said you must realize technology is changing rapidly. What you study and know today may not be relevant in two years. Your college education is a great base, but you need to continually learn new things in technology from your first job until the day you retire. Also, when it comes to specific technology, don't say you're skill is specific to a brand, such as "I am an Avid editor", or indicate your expertise is on a particular system or type of software. That's like saying you're a Makita carpenter or a KitchenAid chef. Don't define yourself by the tools you use. If you're an editor, you should be capable of learning and using most any editing software. Likewise, if you're a cook you should be able to cook with any brand of utensil or oven. That makes a lot of sense! Doesn't it?

READ AS MUCH AS YOU CAN

Another great way to stay relevant in your industry is through reading (and joining industry associations or networking groups). I recommend the great books below. It is imperative you stay up on the latest trends, issues and topics in your industry at all costs. Whether through blogs, internet, magazines, or conversations, you've got to know what's going on in your industry.

Here are a few motivational books that will literally change your life: *How to Stop Worrying and Start Living* by Dale Carnegie is one of the greatest books I ever read. It changed my life dramatically. It will give you perspective on life and tools to overcome worry that will be valuable to you forever. I would say it's the greatest book I ever read prior to reading the Bible, which I now think is the greatest book I ever read.

How to Win Friends and Influence People by Dale Carnegie, *Think and Grow Rich* by Napoleon Hill, *The Dream Giver* by Bruce Wilkerson, and *Seizing Your Divine Moment* by Erwin McManus are examples of other great motivational life books I love. Yes, these are old books... but they work!

Now back to business. Billionaire Warren Buffett is probably regarded as one of the most successful business guys in the world. He says his greatest investment is his investment in himself and reading. He has a favorite business book, a book he thinks is a great book, and it's also Bill Gates' favorite book. The name of the book is **Business Adventures** by John Brooks. Now let me ask you a question. Wouldn't you think it's a good idea to read a book that Warren Buffett thinks is a great book if you wanted to be an investor or businessman? Absolutely, it would be! And, there are other great books you should read as well.

Here are many great books I believe every business person should read:

- *The Effective Executive* by Peter Drucker
- *Good to Great* by Jim Collins
- *Giants of Enterprise* by Richard Tedlow
- *True North: Discover Your Authentic Leadership* by Bill George and Peter Sims
- *Ignore Everybody: and 39 Other Keys to Creativity* by Hugh McLeod
- *Leadership & Self-deception: Getting Out of the box* by Arbinger Institiute
- *Thinking, Fast and Slow* by Daniel Kahneman
- *The Power of Habit* by Charles Duhigg
- *The Wisdom of Failure* by Laurence Weinzimmer and Jon McConoughey
- *The Hard Thing about Hard Things* by Ben Horowitz
- *Zero to One* by Peter Thiel
- *The Lean Startup* by Eric Ries
- *The 4-hour Workweek* by Timothy Ferriss
- *Rework* by Jason Fried and David Heinemeier Hansson
- *The E-Myth Revisited* by Michael Gerber
- *The Alchemist* by Paulo Coelho
- *The $100 Startup* by Chris Guillebeau
- *Delivering Happiness: A Path to Profits, Passion and Purpose* by Tony Hsieh

- *The Millionaire Fastlane* by MJ Demarco
- *Purple Cow (Transform your business by being remarkable)* by Seth Godin
- *Mastery* by Robert Greene
- *Influence: The Psychology of Persuasion* by Robert Cialdini
- *Crush It* by Gary Vaynerchuk
- *Awaken the Giant Within* by Tony Robbins
- *Outliers (The story of success)* by Malcolm Gladwell
- *Rich Dad Poor Dad* by Robert Kiyosaki
- *Art of War* by Sun Tzu
- *The Hard Sell* by Colin Clark and Trevor Pinch
- *Jack: Straight from the Gut* by Jack Welch and John Byrne
- *In Businesses as in Life, You Don't Get What You Deserve, You Get What You Negotiate* by Chester Karrass
- *Little Red Book of Selling* by Jeffrey Gitomer
- *The Art of Strategy* by Avinash Dixit and Barry Nalebuff
- *The Little Engine That Could* (I know this is a children's book, but I love the "can-do" message.) by Watty Piper and Loren Long
- *What They Don't Teach You at Harvard Business School* by Mark McCormack

This is a lot of information for you, and that's just business. If you're a teacher, an astronomer, a photographer, or a painter, you need to read and learn from every book in that industry. You need to study it all. I can't stress this enough. So many people have gone down the road you are traveling. Do not be stubborn, and do not think you can't learn from the wisdom and experiences of these people. I encourage you to set a goal to read at least one to two of these books per month.

FIND MENTORS

In addition to reading as many books as possible about your industry, you should talk to the old-timers, those who have gone before you.

There were some guys at NW Ayer Advertising who were over the hill. I remember one guy in particular named Jules Green, who clearly had a position that didn't require him to work. The industry had possibly passed him by, but, based on his friendships or relationships, he still had a job with the agency. What a resource he was and what knowledge and wisdom he had.

Go out to lunch with old-timers like Jules, or at least take five minutes to pick their brains. The information you'll get is invaluable. It turned out that Jules was a close personal friend of Sammy Cahn, the legendary lyricist and Broadway songwriter, and thus Jules had Sammy write many of the jingles for our clients ad campaigns. This would be the equivalent today of Bruce Springsteen or another major pop star writing your jingle. So you can see Jules' connections made him very valuable to the agency and insured he had job security.

Once I broke through Jules' tough demeanor, and he saw I was genuinely interested in him, he poured some time into me to help mentor me. This is critical again because you don't know the connections the guy has. He can take a liking to you, he can place one good word for you, and your career can leap far ahead. Even if that's not the benefit that comes from it, just picking his brain and getting his knowledge, wisdom and insight is well worth it.

On the subject of mentors, you don't go up to somebody and say, "Will you mentor me?" That sounds like a lifetime commitment and most people are too busy to make that commitment. As a matter of fact, they would dread it. And since they don't know you very well yet, how do they know they really want to mentor you? So, that's not how you get it started.

Here's what you do. You go up to somebody in your office who you would like to get some advice from and say, "Listen, I was just wondering if you can spend five minutes with me. I have a couple of questions I would like to ask you. I'm new in the agency (or new in the business), and I was wondering if I could get the benefit of your experience on a specific issue or two."

Well, of course, that sounds easy. Giving somebody five minutes of my time is no big deal. You're not asking me to commit to meeting with you monthly or be your mentor or plug in to your life. Who doesn't want to be asked their opinion on things and have it valued? So it will also be a big ego play for the guy that you're coming to him for expertise and advice. Then you go in and ask a simple question, something like, "Hey, I'm just starting out and I was wondering, if you look back on your career, what advice would you give me as a guy starting out today here in the agency?" And then shut up and listen because you want to hear what the guy has to say.

Then ask, "Are there ways to get ahead quicker in the agency? Is there more I can do?" Then again, just shut up and listen to what he has to say. Then I would thank him for his time and go about my way.

Now, perhaps in a couple of weeks or a month later, go back in and say, "Hey, I'm just wondering, I have another question or issue I was wondering how to deal with. Could I possibly have five more minutes of your time?" You start to build up this relationship where they want to plug in and mentor you.

Not everybody may become your mentor overnight, not everybody may want to plug in to your life. That's okay. Your job is to build relationships in the agency (or your company) so you can get ahead. You will not necessary mesh or merge with everybody's personality. You may ask for advice from one guy, and he gives you an answer, but he's not your cup of tea. That's okay. You will find someone who is, and you will find people who mentor you even though you never had to ask. It will just happen naturally, and that's the way you want it to be. Those relationships will just develop over time.

Also, as I've told you, if you're playing on the company softball team and the executives are on the softball team, that's a good way to get close to them. If you're involved in working on their charity campaigns, or helping them in other corporate ways after you have completed your own assignments and your own work better than anybody else, you'll naturally get closer to them.

Also, it's great to know other people from other departments. If you're a copywriter, hang out with some of the account management people, the media people, the traffic people. If you're in a factory on the production line, hang out with some of the engineers or some of the people in shipping. Don't limit yourself to the department you're in. See the overall corporate big picture.

TIMING IS EVERYTHING!

Timing is everything in business and in life. I don't walk into a guy's office when he's got a phone to his ear, two people standing there and I see he's under pressure and rushed. That's not the time to ask him if he's got five minutes to give me insight and wisdom into life and business. No! I want to be there at seven in the morning when nobody's in the office, and he's having his coffee and reading his paper, quietly and privately.

You need to know timing. It's something I teach my kids and talk to employees about all the time.

Like when my kids want me to take them for ice cream. They come in and they see I just got off a conference call, and I'm extremely tense. I've got five thousand things on my desk, but they still ask me to take them. I look at them and go, "Not now, kids. I'm really busy." It's the truth, and they're not getting any ice cream. But had they waited a couple of hours, maybe I just got off a great call, I just made some money on a deal, and I'm happy, excited, and laughing. They ask the same question, but now I'm excited to go with them. Now is a good time for me. So, the same exact request can get a completely different response, depending on timing.

At the office, you may get a different answer to the same question based on timing. You need to be able to read people and timing. Understand there is a time and a place for everything. I always like to get the executive before or after business hours or out of the office, like at lunch or coffee.

They reason is he obviously won't get distracted by the phone and other issues of the day. So, before work and after work is ideal. If you're in the office, ask if you can just talk to him for five minutes, or ask to grab a quick cup of coffee outside the office.

Remember, you're going to talk to the old-timers and people in other departments because you want to learn more about the business and how it functions. You're going to read industry magazines and stay up on the topics that are relevant—trends, topics and issues in your industry—so you know what's going on. You want to ask for advice, guidance, and training, but you want to time everything right. Timing is everything.

TAKE⚡ACTION

- Find that technology or idea in your field that you are currently fuzzy on. Track down some books or other info and nail it down. Staying ahead of the technological curve will give you the leg up in today's market. Which magazine(s) can you subscribe to? What articles can you read on the internet?

- Define yourself by the work you do, not by the tools you use. Get knowledgeable with other tools so that you can do your work well no matter which brand of tools you're using. In other words, don't be a "KitchenAid chef" —be a chef.

- Pick, say, two books on the list I provided in the chapter and buy them today. When you're finished with them, buy and read two more. Reading as much as you can will keep you sharp and focused.

- Identify someone you work with right now who has more experience and wisdom. It could even be someone many consider "over the hill." Invite him or her to coffee or lunch this week (make sure that you pay!) and pick their brain. You may be stunned at the things you can learn.

- Think about someone whose work you respect in your workplace and ask them if you could sit down with them for five minutes and ask some questions. A few weeks or a month later, ask them again, and have more questions ready. Over time, you may well have a mentor, and you will almost certainly pick up valuable advice.

• Early in the day and late in the day—outside the crush of the busiest times—is usually when potential mentors are most available to talk to you.

• Get involved in workplace extracurricular activities—after you've seen to it that your work is done impeccably. Invest your time in showing up in strategic places to meet or be around the right people both at your office and in your industry.

CHAPTER 9

KEEP IT REAL

DON'T BE AFRAID TO ASK

Utilize your connections now, not when you're dead. What do I mean? I mean, whether it's family, friends, or business relationships, I have the philosophy that, look, when I die, don't even send flowers to my funeral. You don't even need to attend my funeral. You don't have to do anything. But, if you can help me when I'm alive, that's great because that's when I need your help. However, many people never ask for it. What is the harm in asking?

Another great lesson from my dad— regarding him and other people. He always told me to ask for anything. The worst somebody can do is to say no. If they said no, I would be back in the same exact position as when I started. No worse, no better, so I had nothing to lose. But if they said yes, I was way ahead. Many times, people said yes.

The point is, use your contacts now. What does that mean? If a family member, friend, or business contact can do you a favor, get you an introduction, get you an interview, connect you with someone who may be beneficial to your career, ask them to do it (at the right time, of course!). The worst they could do is say no. If they do say no, do not be upset with them, do not be mad at them, do not take it personally. That's not what this is about.

You can ask like this, "I know you know Dave Smith. Is there any way you could arrange for me to give Dave a phone call? I really want to ask him some advice. I know he's an advertising executive, and I'm getting into advertising (or whatever industry you're looking for help in). Is there any way you could just set up a phone call or maybe arrange for me to meet with him for five minutes and pick his brain to get some advice from him? It would be invaluable to me and I'd really appreciate it."

That's simple and not threatening. Either they will say yes or they will say no. But that's how you do it. You leverage your connections. It's like compounding interest. You don't think it's going to amount to anything, but then over time you've made a fortune because the interest compounds and compounds and compounds. What's the sense of having connections if you're not going to use them?

If you die, and you never used the connections, what value were they to you? The key is to use them while you can. Remember, access every connection while you can. As you develop more connections when you move forward in your career, this same philosophy holds true. It doesn't hurt to ask. The worst someone can do is say no. I think you will be very surprised by all the yeses you will get.

Now a brief word about friends. Friends are important. It's better to have five lottery tickets than one lottery ticket. Why? Because it increases your odds of winning. So, as you get older, especially in college and as you get into the business world, your friends can help you tremendously. They don't have to be in the same industry as you, but they may have connections and know people who can help you dramatically. It's a good idea to have a lot of friends.

I don't mean this selfishly, "Oh ha-ha, I can get something from them." Because remember, you're going to give as well. You're going to be a valuable asset to your friends. I hope you will have many genuine, true friendships, relationships, and connections that can help you down the line. This is an extremely valuable commodity. You may have heard the old saying "It's not about what you do. It's about who you know." Well, that's true!

You can certainly make it in your business or career based only on talent and what you do. That may take you a certain amount of time. You can also do it based on who you know and who can get you there quicker, and that may take you a shorter time, which will be better. That's a valuable weapon and tool.

I don't think a carpenter would go to a job with just a hammer. No, he has nails, a screwdriver, a drill gun, a saw, and all the rest of his tools. So, you, as a business person, looking to succeed in your career, need to have all the tools. People are valuable tools. Talent is a valuable tool. Determination is a valuable tool. Integrity is a valuable tool. And you combine them all. Maybe you have some more than others, but you should have all of them and work at getting better and more skilled at using all of them.

Now let me go even a step further. I would make friends that I needed. Hey, I'm not too particularly proud of this, but in my drug days in college and just after I got out of college, I was still partying a little too much. I was on a softball team and one of the guys was a doctor. I went out of my way to become friends with him. I mean, I made it a point to become friends with him because I thought it was beneficial for me. And it was. So, I say the same thing to you. You can make it a point to pick particular people you want to be friends with. Particular people can help advance and influence your career in a dramatic way, and, yes, you're going to have to invest in those friendships. You're not going to get away with being phony and just thinking somebody is going to like you because you shake their hand.

You're going to have to put in time and effort to go above and beyond. They're not all going to work out, and they're not all going to want to be your friends. But some of them will and you just need one of them to work out. Remember my dad's saying—you just need one guy to like you, one guy to say yes. You just need one guy to come in and mentor you, one guy to connect you where you need to be connected. You may have many, but you need at least one.

Friends, contacts, and connections are important. You should mine them and invest in them like you would in anything else. They're a great tool.

CHOOSE AN EMPOWERING PERSPECTIVE

For every guy in the NBA today playing basketball, there are thousands of kids who will never make it. For every Mark Zuckerberg who started Facebook, there are a thousand broke kids living in the family's garage or attic thinking they're going to be the next technological billionaire, and they're not! It doesn't mean you shouldn't go for it, though. It doesn't mean you shouldn't strive to be that guy.

It just means you want to be realistic and you want to

know what you need to do to give yourself every edge and advantage. Then do it. You execute the plays as best you can without concern for the outcome. The outcome will take care of itself. But if I'm five feet four, the chances of me getting into the NBA are pretty slim, so perhaps that's not the career for me. I need to evaluate my talents and strengths and use them accordingly.

I remember walking into Henry Kornhauser's office-the CEO at Kornahuser and Calene, the agency I worked at after NW Ayer—one day and he said, "Son, let's have a chat." I was dating his daughter at the time (a wonderful girl who I really loved), and I think he wanted to impart some life wisdom into me. He said, "Things will never be perfect. Something will always be wrong either with your health, a relationship, money, children, wife, or business. Something in your life will always be wrong."

I looked at him as a twenty-three-year-old kid, and I said, "You're out of your mind. You're crazy. That's so sad." I thought life was great, and we should always enjoy it. There doesn't always have to be something wrong.

I learned later he was the voice of experience talking. I had youth on my side with a lot of excitement and optimism. He had traveled down life's road for over sixty years, so his version of reality was a lot different than mine. I soon came to see that perhaps he wasn't so foolish after all.

Indeed, as life went on it seemed something was always wrong in some area. But that's okay. I think it's just a perspective issue and how you look at it. Maybe he was right about something always being wrong, but he wasn't right about not being happy all the time even when everything is not going our way. If you're smart you learn to roll with life and enjoy the ride.

Baseball players don't get a hit every time up.

Quarterbacks don't complete every pass, but they love playing the game. I think that's the difference. You have to love being alive. You have to love living. You can find a lot of reasons to be miserable. You can look at any category of your life and find something not going your way and be miserable because of it.

I choose to look at life the other way. I choose to look at life as a gift. Being alive is a wonderful, special privilege. Thus, if I look at any area in my life that isn't going exactly as I want, that's okay. It's just great to be alive and in the game!

On a side note. At a different ad agency, I was dating the chairman of the board's secretary. As such, we were getting Broadway tickets, limousines, dinners out, and a variety of other perks and benefits that were available to her as secretary to the head of the agency that would never have been available to me as a rising young account executive. I did not date her for that reason, but that was one of the perks that came along with it.

When I was dating Henry Kornhauser's daughter, that brought even more benefits with it, both personally and professionally. It brought me to a closer relationship with the boss, who brought me into his inner circle, allowing me to hear his thinking and strategy. He blessed me with extra benefits, including money.

He wound up investing in my ad agency in Florida and launching me in that venture. Now I did not date his daughter to gain any business advantage. I genuinely cared for her. Nor would I say that you should do that in order to advance your career. However, if things happen to work out that way, it is not a bad thing.

MOTIVATE YOURSELF

All through my career I was motivated, determined, focused, single-minded, and would do whatever it took to get the job done, remembering it was not about a timetable. It was about accomplishing the goal. So I often challenge myself by thinking this way when I'm facing a tough obstacle or something I don't want to do. I ask myself this question. If a person or company came in right now and offered me $1 million to do this particular job or task, would I do it? Even if I didn't enjoy it, even if I didn't want to do it, would I do it? Think of something you don't want to do, but would do if you got paid to do it. Would I make sales calls? Stay the course on a difficult unpleasant assignment or task until it was done? Do something I didn't particularly enjoy?

Of course the answer is yes, for million dollars I would do it. That's great... so the truth of the matter is, I can do it! Now the question is am I willing to do it for myself? It boggles my mind that people will do things they don't want to do when people pay them to do it, but when it's for themselves and their own best interests, they can't get motivated to do what it takes to get the job done and get ahead. I think that's tragic!

When I was in New York, my buddy Frank and I started a company. I thought he would be an ideal guy to do sales and marketing for this company. I had a concept I thought would work very well, and I knew Frank had been successful in sales before. He was a top sales producer, and I knew he would be the perfect guy to do sales for my company and allow me to focus on management and developing the product.

We started a company together, fifty-fifty partners. We were doing our roles and when it came down to it, Frank was really unable to perform his role. I thought he would be aggressive and do whatever it took to get the job done and be the best kick-ass salesman, as he had been for a previous company.

So, I was surprised, astounded, because I knew he had the talent and the ability, yet I saw he was just unable, or unwilling, to do it. And I realized then that he wasn't able to do it for himself. The fact that he had an ownership and equity position in our company wasn't enough drive to motivate him. However, he stood to make millions of dollars in this company.

He stood to set himself up financially for life and be way ahead of the game. This was a golden opportunity for him, and all he had to do was his job. I was paying all of the financial expenses of the company and if we succeeded, we would both be very well off. Yet he functioned outstandingly in operations. He was a great detail man, and a great guy. I love him to this day but he was unable to perform in the sales role—the key role we needed most.

It was almost as if he was frozen and paralyzed. He couldn't or wouldn't do it. One day I told him I was really surprised since he'd done this before for other companies. He'd made six figures doing it. I knew he was trying to secure a financial future for his family and he was concerned about that but he had a six-month financial cushion so he could plow into this company with all his effort.

I told him I knew if I had come along and offered him a huge salary plus big commissions to be my sales guy for the company, he'd be kicking butt. However, now when he owned half of it and could make himself millions of dollars, he couldn't motivate himself to do it. Even after that talk, he was unable to dig down deep and do whatever it took. That doesn't make him a bad person. As a matter of fact, Frank is a wonderful guy and one of my dearest friends.

I just shared this with you for motivational purposes. Make sure you do whatever it takes to get yourself motivated! I also shared this to tell you that it's amazing to me that, if other people pay us, we're motivated. We'll do whatever it takes. But when it's our own best interests, sometimes we can't get motivated and do it. I think that's ridiculous.

Remind yourself you need to work and perform as if somebody is paying you well. If you're looking for a job and you can't get motivated to look for a job, I'll tell you what, if I paid you $200,000 a year, $4,000 a week, and your job was to look for a job, you'd be looking really hard. So the question isn't can you do it... It's will you! So, whatever it takes to motivate yourself, you have to do it. That's important.

TAKE ACTION

• Don't be afraid to ask for something. The worst thing that can happen is someone will tell you no. You'll survive it and they will often say yes.

• Cultivate friends and relationships. Seek their help, and be willing to help them in return. This is different than playing office politics. This means really making solid connections that you can go back and forth with for the rest of your life. Nothing will be more valuable to you.

• Events happen to you, but you choose how you are going to view them and handle them. Decide that you are not going to be a victim, but instead see every day as a gift no matter how difficult the results it brings you.

• Don't wait for others to come along and inspire and motivate you. Set goals, dream big and keep focused on what you need to do to motivate and inspire yourself to success. Learn how to motivate yourself. It will make you a fortune.

• Find the thing in your work—or in your life goals— to motivate you to give one hundred percent today. Be specific about what you want and run with it.

• Are you leveraging your connections? Most everyone you need to know is already in your phone or e-mail contacts. Is there is a family member, friend or business connection who can help get you an introduction to the right person, secure an interview at your dream company or connect you with someone who may be beneficial to your career? Ask them to help this week.

CHAPTER 10

LOOK AT EVERY ANGLE

SNAPSHOT

1. Discover the incredible power of flexibility and creativity to generate desired outcomes.

2. Understand the importance of thinking on your feet and looking for every angle to reach success.

3. Learn how important it is for people to like you. It's amazing how much more they will do for you when they like you and believe in you.

My dad would call people up when he owned a small wholesale paper supply company. He'd say, "I know you have a main supplier. Use me as a secondary, back-up guy. If you need an emergency delivery or have an order too small for you regular guy to send a truck out to deliver, call me. I'll do it." Of course, Dad knew once he got his foot in the door with a company, he would win them over and get more and more business if not their entire account. It was out of the box, strategic thinking.

Some of the greatest lessons I learned in business happened when I got involved in a renewable energy project. We were attempting to permit and build what was at that time the largest solar farm in the country, a 70 MW solar farm in Hamilton County, Florida. (This was the HERO solar project I told you about in chapter 4.)

I walked into this opportunity, not by choice. I was involved as the lead investor in a five-hundred-acre piece of land in Hamilton County. Then, the real estate (and stock) market crashed, and we were looking for ways to save the land as we really thought it was a jewel and had great potential value.

I worked out a deal to cash out all of the original investors who were crushed and losing their money. They wanted out because they desperately needed cash because all their other investments were crashing and burning at the same time. I wanted to bring in new investors to save the land. Of course, this was a partially selfish desire on my part as I did not want to get wiped out, and I believed in the future potential of the land. I was trying to create a win-win scenario for all parties involved.

Out of desperation I looked for alternative uses for the land. I ran a Hail Mary play. Hey, it works in football, why not in business? So I ran an ad in Barron's financial newspaper. It cost me two thousand dollars for a three-line ad to run one time. I advertised I was looking for investors for a solar or wind farm in Florida thinking perhaps this could be a good use for the land. Of course, I didn't know what I was doing in either of those fields and soon learned that you didn't put wind farms in Florida because there isn't enough wind in the Sunshine State to make it viable. But, solar could definitely work.

Most people who responded to the ad hung up on me when they realized that I didn't know what I was doing or talking about. But one guy was willing to walk me through the process and guide me. His name was Steve O'Brien from California. He gently and kindly took me step by step through the process and guided me. Remember, I knew nothing about solar. I didn't know the technology or the terms, and I do not consider myself to be a science or engineering guy. None of that appeals to me. Yet, in order to go forward I had to learn quickly.

I did what I always do. I dug in and focused on the task at hand. We started to work with an engineer, Dr.

Tom Damberger out of California, a wonderful man who believed in me so much that he was kind enough to tie his compensation into the future success of the project. I asked questions left and right, day and night.

We went to a trade show, and I walked up and down the aisle, asking questions about technology and then asking the same question again and again until I finally began to understand. That's what it takes for me to learn. I have to see and understand and process it in my brain until I'm sure I've got it. I also wasn't scared to look like an idiot. I wasn't scared to feel foolish. I needed to get that information, and I didn't care how I had to do it.

I started to learn all about renewable energy and, specifically, solar project development. I started to learn about interconnect agreements with utility companies and the technology and process involved there. And, believe me, it is a bureaucracy. They are guided by FERC (Federal Energy Regulatory Commission) guidelines as well as their own utility and state regulations.

Then, I had to delve into politics, as we needed to lobby the state of Florida's politicians to come up with enticements and tax benefits to make it so the project would be worth building. It's one thing to get a permit for an interconnection agreement, but it's another thing if it doesn't make financial sense to build it. I had to go down both roads simultaneously. The interconnect agreement process consisted of three separate studies, $160,000 in deposits and about a year and a half to go through the process. I found myself up in Tallahassee learning how the lobbying game operates. It operates like this—you give them all your money and pray! (Smile!)

I met with senators, congressmen, the governor, and his energy czar, as well as the Florida agricultural commissioner and anybody who could possibly help us. The idea of exemptions and tax benefits and credits for solar energy was running rampant. We hired lobbyists, and I learned to effectively play in this arena. It wasn't one I particularly enjoyed, by the way, because no matter what the politicians tell you or say, at the end of the day they just do whatever they want! What a learning experience.

Part of me was sure these guys were operating like organized crime, saying whatever they wanted and then doing whatever they wanted without any regard for the outcome except to line their own pockets.

Not all were like that, of course. I met a very few who really seemed to want to do what was best for the people in the state, but they were few and far between. I quickly realized the politics side of it was a game I could not win, and I was out of my league. Although it was fascinating to spend a couple of years learning the ins and outs.

I was able to convince Schneider Electric, one of the largest suppliers of solar equipment and EPC (Engineering, Procurement and Construction) contractors in the world, to work on our project. We needed design plans for our solar farm and substation. I was able to convince them by meeting with their top executives (about nine of them in the room at once with just me, Steve O'Brien and Tom Damberger) that they should put in over $100,000 worth of design work for free.

If we were successful, we would buy their equipment and use them for construction. However, if we were not successful, we would owe them nothing. I'll never forget Mike Rice, the Schneider executive who was in charge of making the decision at that point saying, "I like you guys and we'll take a shot on you." Indeed, Schneider did the design work at no cost.

It didn't hurt that I rearranged my schedule a few weeks prior to meet with Mike when he was in Miami. I drove down and spent a few hours with him getting to know him on a one-to-one basis.

I can't tell you how many conference calls I was on with the Progress Energy, now Duke Energy, utility interconnect team, their engineers, and Schneider engineers over the years. So much so that I soon became very familiar with solar terminology and technology. How scary is that? But it had to be done.

The good news is we got the project permitted and signed an interconnect agreement with the utility. Then, using some technicalities, and availing ourselves of every loophole and option that would benefit us while always staying within the confines of the game—remember, I said you need to beat the system, but always from within—we were able to extend our interconnect agreement hoping for a favorable economic climate to get the project built.

We called the project the Hercules Solar Project, and our company was HERO Solar. I'm extremely proud of the relationships we built during the project, the people we came in contact with, and the lives we were able to influence both on a spiritual and business basis. Many of the people I met are still my friends today.

Why do I share this with you? To tell you that I use the same principles in every aspect of my business that I use when I'm going into something new and unknown. I'm determined to work harder and smarter, looking for every angle. I'm determined to make and leverage relationships with people that will pay off in a big way. This formula has paid off for me in everything I've ever done. Use it and it will pay off for you as well.

TAKE ACTION

- Look at potential barriers between you and where you want to be. Think about how you can approach them from another angle.

- Question everything about the barrier, including the things you take for granted. For me, it was a piece of land and how I could use it differently. For you, perhaps it's a relationship you need to adjust, or a door you need to knock on. Look for every angle!

- If you're having trouble finding a new angle or barriers are in your way, you need to know more about them. Learn more. Be willing to ask questions, look for articles, read books, and anything else you can do to know everything you can about it, which is where you'll find the new angle!

- Leverage your relationships to help you discover angles and opportunities you may have missed.

- When a situation seems hopeless, don't be afraid to throw a "Hail Mary" pass. What can it hurt?

CHAPTER 11
STAY IN THE GAME

SNAPSHOT

1. Discover the importance of perseverance to your short and long-term success.

2. Learn to focus on completing the task at hand with excellence. That trait will serve you very well over time.

3. Understand why quitting is not an option.

This is probably one of the most important things I can teach you. It's a life lesson and a business lesson. You need to get this and understand this. You need to stay in the game no matter what. You need to keep going even when you can't see victory, even when you think you've been defeated, even when you're knocked down. You need to keep going.

Do not quit. In chess, if you knock down your king, it means you quit; the game is over. I've seen great comebacks in sports. I've seen the New York Yankees come back from being down sixteen games at the All-Star break one year and win the American League Championship. I've seen the Buffalo Bills in a playoff game against the Houston Oilers down thirty-two points in the third quarter. Frank Reich a replacement quarterback, came in to take over for the star quarterback. He rallied that team to victory in the second half of that game.

They had no chance. They were beaten, defeated, completely done for, yet they kept playing, one play at a time. One down at a time, they rallied and won the game. It's the same thing in life and business. Your job is to keep playing until the clock ticks zero. You don't worry about how much time is left, even if you're down ten to two in the ninth inning in baseball. You don't quit. You take your bat and keep swinging, and you know what? You can come back and win.

I'm not saying you win every time. I'm saying when you quit, you never win. You're done. So, we don't quit. We keep going no matter what. I can't tell you how many times in my life I have come out ahead simply because I didn't quit, even when I wanted to.

I remember a couple of instances—one in particular. In ninth grade they were giving Regents Exams (a requirement at that time in New York State) that played an important part in college admissions. I knew there was no chance I would pass the Regents Exams for math and science that year. I was not a fan of algebra and chemistry as I always knew my future was in business. I didn't know the material and that was going to be a problem for me. But, I signed up to take the test anyway, figuring I would just keep going and see what happened.

Believe it or not, the test got stolen for the year (I didn't steal it) and they gave everybody that signed up a passing grade. So, get this right. Just because I signed up, I got a passing grade! Just because I kept going until the clock ticked zero. Those who did not sign up to take the test did not receive the credit. I kept going until that clock ticked zero.

At Syracuse University, when I was a student, I didn't want to take a college math class. I really didn't like math as you can tell. I passed algebra and trigonometry in high school by the skin of my teeth, but a math class was a requirement for college graduation. So, I found a way out.

I found an angle out. I did some research, and I learned that you can actually petition the dean of your school. Previously, I didn't know you could petition the dean. You can actually submit a written petition to the dean of the school to change a requirement or have an exception made in a certain cases. You could ask for anything! It didn't mean you would get it, but there was no restriction on what you could ask for.

I wrote an eloquent and well thought out petition to the dean. In essence it said, "I'm an advertising guy. I don't need math. I will be better served by taking this other marketing class." He approved it for me. He changed the rules and approved my request. Had I not had the diligence and desire to find the answer and the way out, had I just accepted what was put in front of me, had I just quit and stopped, that never would have happened.

Another time, I had a large amount of restricted stock in a public company. Restricted stock means you can't sell it until a particular time period has elapsed and then only certain quantities at a time. The stock didn't trade a lot. There was not much value or interest in the stock, and I wasn't sure the company would make it, but I had millions of dollars in that company's stock and there was a strong possibility it would be worthless down the line.

Again, I did my research. I checked and found you are allowed to donate restricted stock and take a tax deduction (as long as you pay to get independent appraisal of the stock, which I did). So, rather than wait to see if the stock was up or down, I donated a large portion of it at that time and got a serious tax deduction. That move, finding out, doing research, probably made me a million dollars because I looked for the angle. I looked for the legal loophole and way out. Even when I was stopped, I kept going, I kept looking for the way to succeed. That is a key to victory. You don't quit. You keep playing.

In basketball, if you're down twenty points late in the game, you don't say we lost. You keep playing the best you can until the clock ticks zero. When the clock ticks zero, if you lost, you've lost. That's okay. But the way you come back, the way you have great comebacks in business, in life, and in sports is you keep playing.

You stay focused on the task at hand. Each individual at bat, each individual play, each individual shot you make with excellence. Don't look at the circumstance and get crushed by that. Don't worry about what happened on the last play or what's going to happen on the next play. Focus on this play, on the task on hand, and do it with excellence.

All of the great sports guys of my day—Jerry Rice, Michael Jordan, Don Mattingly, Wayne Gretzky, Isaiah Thomas, Derek Jeter—day in and day out lived and played with excellence. Business guys are the same way. They live and play with excellence all of their careers. As opposed to one-hit wonders, one-season rookies who have fallen to the sophomore jinx or just the hard reality of maintaining consistency and excellence over a long period of time.

No, it's about continued excellence day in and day out. It's about giving all you have. It's about consistency and excellence. That's how you need to be. That's what you need to strive for. That's what you need to keep doing. Stay in the game no matter what, even when you can't see victory or you think you've been defeated. Keep going.

TAKE ACTION

- Never quit. Even when things look hopeless, there's always a chance. The Buffalo Bills were losing to the Houston Oilers 35-3 in the third quarter—and came back to win! You may not win every time, but when you quit, you can never win.

- Where do you see a potential defeat in your own career or life? Identify it—and then resolve to stay in the game and keep pushing forward regardless.

CHAPTER 12

PREPARE TO WIN

SNAPSHOT

1. Discover the critical importance of preparation and a willingness to learn from others to achieve success in business.

2. Understand why it is vital that you act and not react when facing challenges in business.

3. Learn how failure can actually help you reach success.

Remember, you want to follow instructions. You want to learn from people who have done it. Why do baseball players still have hitting coaches when they know how to hit? Why do actors have acting coaches when they know how to act? They do it to keep their skills sharp.

When Dow Chemical, the creator and manufacturer of a popular lawn bug killer, says mix half a cup of chemical with every gallon of water you should listen. If you don't listen, if you use six cups, you're going to kill your lawn. I'm telling you from personal experience!

I thought I had bugs in my lawn that needed to die. So, when Dow Chemical said to use half a cup of their product, I figured my bugs were the worst, so I'd use six cups. I burned out my whole lawn. All I had to do was follow the simple instructions, but I was stubborn, prideful, and thought I knew better than the manufacturer and creator. Let me tell you, that did not work well!

I have learned that following instructions and learning from people who know is a good way to get things done. I don't have to repeat mistakes that were already made. So, if I talk to somebody, or read a book, or learn a story of someone who has been down a similar road and I can learn from their experiences, I want to do that. I don't want to be prideful and stubborn. I want to learn so my goals are accomplished faster. I'm not scared to be humble or learn or be in a secondary position if it will get me where I want to go sooner.

Let me give you an example. One time I donated a large sum to a charity and as a result got the opportunity to meet Bruce Springsteen backstage. It was Bruce's sixtieth birthday, and we were going backstage after the concert. We were supposed to call Tom Rye, who was with Bruce's management agency, and Tom would tell us where to meet him after the show and get us back in to see Bruce.

Well, rest assured of one thing, I was going to do whatever Tom Rye told me to do, and I did exactly what he told me to do. I went exactly where he told me to go, walked how he told me to walk, shut up when he told me to shut up, and talked when he told me to talk. Normally, I'm the one giving orders and instructions but no, not this time. I wanted to go where only Tom Rye could take me, and I would have done whatever it took. Remember that. It's okay to be humble. It's okay to listen to somebody else. It's okay to learn from them, especially when they know where they're going and what they're doing, and you don't. You'll learn, and then you'll know.

I think we can learn something from history. Some incredible people have learned some very hard lessons. I read an article by Dan Waldschmidt you can see it on the Success.com website. It was titled "Stop Making Excuses for Who and Where You Are," and it gave examples of some amazingly successful people who had many failures in their lives. Take a look at a few.

- Sigmund Freud was booed off the stage the first time he presented his theories to a group of scientists in Europe. He went on to win the Goethe Award for his work in psychology (and is probably the most famous psychologist ever).

- Winston Churchill failed sixth grade and lost every public election he ran for until he was elected Prime Minister of England at the age of sixty-two. (He became one of the most respected world leaders ever.)

- Albert Einstein didn't speak until he was four years old, couldn't read basic words until he was seven and was expelled from school. He eventually revolutionized physics with his Theory of Relativity.

- Henry Ford failed at farming, at being an apprentice and as a machinist, and went bankrupt five times. He modernized mass production (and became the head of one of the largest auto companies ever, Ford Motors).

- Stan Smith was rejected as a ball boy for a Davis Cup tennis match because he was "too clumsy." He won eight Davis Cup championships and is considered one of the greatest doubles tennis players of all time.

- Charles Schultz had every cartoon rejected that he submitted to his high school yearbook. He was rejected by Walt Disney. He went on to create the most popular cartoon series ever: Peanuts.

- Van Gogh only sold one painting his entire life—to a friend's sister for about $50. He painted over eight hundred masterpieces, seven of which are cumulatively worth almost $1 billion.

- Leo Tolstoy flunked out of law school and was labeled"unable to learn" by his professors. He went on to become one of the world's greatest novelists.

• Hank Aaron failed tryouts for the Brooklyn Dodgers and went 0-5 in his first game in the majors. He went on to set the MLB record for homeruns and held that record for thirty-three years.

But, it's not about them. It's about you. The question is, are you prepared to do what you need to do to be successful? That is the question. Remember this, the beauty of success—whether it is finding the girl of your dreams, the right job, or financial success—it doesn't matter how many times you fail, you only have to be right once. And then everybody can tell you how lucky you are. That's advice from billionaire Mark Cuban. It's great advice. Remember it.

Remember, when you get your driver's license, nobody asks you how many times you took the test to pass. They just want to know if you have it or not. When you're a lawyer and you pass the bar exam, nobody asks how many times you took the bar exam before you passed. They just want to know if you passed it. That's all that matters.

It's the same thing in life and success. You just have to be right once, but you have to be in it to win it. You've got to swing the bat to hit the ball, and that's what it's all about. Stay in the game. Keep moving forward.

Just imagine this. It's the bottom of the ninth inning in a baseball game. It's two outs, the bases are loaded, and your team is trailing by a run. A player gets up to hit, the pitcher throws the ball and it's strike one, right down the middle of the plate. The batter does not swing. Next pitch comes, right down the middle of the plate, the batter doesn't swing—strike two.

The next pitch comes. Again, right down the middle of the plate, but the batter's bat is motionless, on his shoulder, he does not swing. Strike three you're out! The team loses. The game is over. The crowd is going wild screaming at the batter, calling him a bum. Understand this, the crowd wouldn't be mad at the guy if he swung and missed. They wouldn't be mad at the guy if he swung and hit the ball and somebody caught it. They're mad at the guy because he didn't even swing. He didn't even try. He had the opportunity to try, and he didn't try. That's why we gave him the bat...to use it! That's your life. Swing!

What if the batter was scared? What if he struck out yesterday? What if he was scared about tomorrow? Yet he was in that moment in that time and should have swung at that pitch. Win, lose, or draw, he should have swung at that pitch. And that's your life.

You have this life to use. Go for it. Don't sit there and be scared. You need to swing. Go for the opportunities and take chances to get ahead. Nobody will be mad at you for not succeeding, but they will be furious at you for not trying. Tony Robbins, one of the great motivators and marketing guys of our time, uses a very simple theory to motivate people. I'm drilling it down to its very basic premise, which is how he gets people to walk across fiery coals and do things they would never do. They break through life obstacles and have these breakthrough lives.

He basically said to think about all these things you fear—asking the girl out, starting the new business, taking a different job with a new company, taking a chance, going to live your dream and being as successful as you really want to be. Think about all those things you're not doing that you really want to do but don't or won't because of fear, concern, or lack of confidence.

Now, imagine you are eighty years old. You're sitting on your back porch and you never did those things. You never asked a girl out. You never got married and had kids. You never left your job because you were scared that you might not make it on your own. You never started your business. You never got wealthy, and you never had a retirement life you could enjoy. You were always a prisoner working under somebody else's thumb and hating it.

How does that feel? And, of course, everybody says that's terrible—the reality and realization that basically, you no longer have that opportunity, you're too old to pursue your dreams, it's over, you've in essence wasted that at bat. You struck out and have nothing. Imagine the pain of that. Imagine the regret and shame and pain you will feel in your heart.

Hold on to that pain. Hold on to that feeling. Now imagine you did ask the girl out, you did start the business. Maybe it worked and maybe it didn't work, (hopefully it did, in which case you are the happiest person in the world) but either way, you went for it. You tried it. You did it! Now you're sitting there, eighty years old, and there's no regret.

Which pain would be worse—the pain of the girl saying no, of having started the business or followed your dream and passion and having it not work out? Or would it be worse sitting there on the porch never having tried? And, of course, every person, one hundred percent of them, say it would be worse to have never tried. That's right.

So, Tony Robbins in essence says, "Now with that in mind, go and live your dreams and purpose." And, of course, people do. They are motivated to change and go and do because they are able to project what would happen if they hadn't. That's what you need to do. You need to realize that and go for it.

I read another article by Melissa Burns, which appeared in Inc. magazine called "Entrepreneurs Tell How They Bounce Back from Setbacks." She looks at what some great entrepreneurs have said about the impact of setbacks in their life.

Gary Vaynerchuk, a social media guru and author, once said, "I lost millions in revenue overnight when states changed the laws effectively stopping us from shipping to those states period. The only thing that got me through and continues to get me through anything is the desire to help others and protect the well-being of my family. If you ever lose perspective and think this is more important than your family, ask yourself, what if this business situation worked out perfectly, but the people you cared about the most are going through health issues or suffering in pain?"

Barbara Corcoran, a real estate guru, said, "I had twenty-two jobs and was fired from seven of them before starting my business. If I had been successful at any of those jobs, I wouldn't have become self-employed. When my boyfriend and business partner left me to marry my secretary, I was devastated. When I finally ended our business partnership, he told me I would never succeed without him. I did and sold my new business for sixty-six million dollars years later. On the heels of every setback is an equally large comeback. If you're smart enough to hang in there and find it."

Jay Georgi the founder of Nadvia Diversified Solutions said this, "Huge failures make you realize who your friends are. I fell seven times back to back, then went bankrupt and hit rock bottom. I lost millions investing and was removed as CEO of my own fund. I once got rejected fifty-two times in sixty days. Each failure taught me resilience, persistence and what not to do." Failure is just an event. It will pass. It's not permanent."

Rafe Furst, co-founder of Crowdfunder, said this, "In life, generally, but in entrepreneurship especially, many outcomes are beyond your control. The best you can do is tip the odds in your favor by making good decisions. Just because you fail at doing something does not make you a failure. Remember, being good has nothing to do with achievement. You are a good person worthy of love and belonging independent of what you achieve or don't achieve."

Billionaire Mark Cuban shared a few of his business lessons "Everyone has the will to win. It's only those that will to prepare that do win", and the other was, "one thing we can all control is effort."

I believe putting in the time to become an expert in whatever you're doing will give you an advantage because most people don't do this. That's critical. I know a guy who became an expert in sleep. He read eight or nine books on sleep and gained a tremendous amount of knowledge on the topic so he became an expert in the area of sleep. If you study and learn, you'll probably be an expert in anything you focus on.

Do not be upset about one bad incident or poor performance in your life. Do not let it define you. The world, your family or friends shouldn't look at you or judge you based on one incident in your life. We don't judge a movie by one scene in the movie. We don't judge a book by one page of the book. And we don't judge you by one incident or circumstance that happened—either good or bad. If people choose to judge you based on one incident, you need to be smart enough to ignore that criticism, as there are some people who will never see the light, who are just judgmental and condemning. Some of them we have to put up with as they are family, but we do not have to let them impact the truth about ourselves.

You may have made some mistakes along the way, and you probably will make more. Those don't define you. A baseball player who struck out in a game, or had a bad week, isn't defined by that. No, his career defines him, his statistics year in and year out define his greatness. Don't get overly focused on one incident of failure in your life. It doesn't define you. At the end of the day, history will record your performance. Your job is to focus on each individual task and do the best you can.

TAKE ACTION

- Follow instructions and listen to the people who know. Why waste a lot of time and cause yourself headaches making mistakes you could've easily avoided?

- Being willing to listen to others takes humility. Is there a place where your pride is causing you to chart your own course when there might be a better way? If so, stop what you're doing and follow those who know!

- Think about the things you are afraid to step out and do. Now, imagine yourself being eighty years old, and not having done those things. Take that feeling, hold onto it, and let it motivate you to move forward. You have one life to live on this earth. Go for the opportunities and take calculated risks to get ahead.

- You only have to be right once in order to be a success. So don't be afraid of being wrong a bunch of times before then! Every successful person has failures behind them.

- Are you replaying one bad incident or poor performance in your mind, allowing it to hold you back? If so, forgive yourself. Ask others to forgive you where appropriate, and begin to focus your thoughts on the opportunities in front of you. Remember, your life will be judged by the whole performance not by one bad scene.

CHAPTER 13

ATTITUDE

SNAPSHOT

1. Discover the importance of thinking outside the box to develop creative solutions that work best for your situation.

2. Understand the connection between your attitude and your ability to achieve desired results quicker.

3. Learn why it's critical to speak up and share your thoughts with company executives and leaders.

I want to share a few stories of doing whatever it takes to get the job done concerning my children. When my son Ricky was fifteen, he was an aspiring saxophone player. I wrote a letter to David Sanborn (one of the greatest sax players in the world at that time), asking him if he would meet with Ricky and give him his input and advice on his future. I told him, of course, I couldn't even put a price on what his time and insight was worth but would appreciate it if he would just consider making an investment in my son's future. Sanborn responded through his manager that he would meet with him and arranged to spend a half hour with Ricky after one of his concerts. Sanborn poured into Ricky's life with invaluable advice regarding music and career.

I did the same thing some fifteen years later for my daughter Talia, who was thirteen at the time and aspiring to be a dancer. She wanted to meet Broadway and YouTube star Todrick Hall. I sent the same type of letter saying that I would appreciate it so much, as a father, if he would invest some time in my daughter. Of course, I said I couldn't pay him for his time—it was worth so much—but would appreciate it if he found it in his heart to carve some time out for her. I knew money wasn't the motivation for these guys, but being able to impact somebody's life usually is. He did and also met us backstage and spent almost an hour pouring into Talia with unbelievable, invaluable advice about the theater and dancing and what it took to succeed.

At the time I wrote him, Todrick Hall was living on a tour bus going from town to town. They were not staying at hotels, so there was no way to directly get to him. I sent a Federal Express overnight letter to the theater in Washington where he was playing the next day. I had to hope that the theater actually got the letter, that they in turn actually gave it to him, and that he actually read it. In essence, I had to hit a moving target. Wouldn't you know it, sure enough the next day I got an e-mail from his assistant to come on down with my daughter and meet him the following week in Florida. It worked!

Both of these things would never have happened if I didn't think outside the box and do whatever it took to get it done. I was highly motivated to bless my children in any way I could. Therefore, I was looking for ways to accomplish what had seemed impossible.

I took a shot. I could have been turned down. They could have not responded, but they did and because my letters were sincere and well thought out, it worked. I thought outside the box and made it happen.

You need to have that same attitude and thought. You need to be an impact player. You need your life to matter. The impact players accomplish things and get things done.

There can be twenty-five guys on a baseball team but not all of them are impact players. As a matter of fact, some of them don't even play a lot. Impact players impact the game, like Lebron James and Tom Brady. A non-impact player is someone who's there but doesn't have any impact on the outcome of the game. You need to be an impact player in your life.

When I first started working at Kornhauser and Calene Advertising, I was working for a man named Kenmore Emerson, who was a straight-laced, corporate guy. He was nice enough but certainly not your warm, fuzzy type. On this one specific account, National Westminster Bank (a large bank at the time) I reported directly to Kenmore on both accounts. He also had another account that we were working on called Spectravideo. It was a new computer company. I worked very hard for Kenmore. I learned from him even though he wasn't the most liked guy in the agency, but I liked him. He was perceived as cozying up to the CEO, which by the way was a very astute career move on Kenmore's part, whether anybody else liked it or not!

I worked my butt off for him. After only being at the agency for a month, based on my work for Spectravideo, Kenmore wrote a letter to Henry Kornhauser, the agency CEO, on my behalf, unsolicited. I didn't even know he had written it. The memo told Henry about the work I had done over the weekend at the trade show, how hard I worked in general, and how much I'd accomplished since I joined the company a short thirty days prior. It told Henry to give me a raise. Henry gave me a five-thousand-dollar raise based on Kenmore's memo! That was pretty impressive. Again, I set that pace. I would do anything and whatever it took, and it paid off instantly. I love when a plan works!

I was the account executive for Spectravideo, and Kenmore was the account supervisor. One time at another trade show Spectravideo was doing a video presentation and some of their equipment failed. They needed a special piece of equipment to work the computer. The pressure was on. The conference and trade show were going to be big failures if they couldn't make their presentation, and I had about thirty minutes to secure a piece of equipment that no one could find because it was not readily available.

I searched the old fashioned way—yellow pages. There was no Google back then. So, I made of ton of urgent phone calls. It was already 5 p.m. and most businesses were closed for the day, but I finally found a company that could actually deliver the equipment in an in hour, so the day was saved. The presentation could go on and that cost was going to be a thousand dollars.

The president of Spectravideo, Harry Fox, said just do whatever it takes to get the piece of equipment over. I got it and was feeling very proud of myself that I had accomplished the impossible in a short period of time. A couple of weeks later, Harry Fox didn't want to pay the bill for that piece of equipment. He said they didn't end up using it anyway so it was unnecessary. I reminded him to his face that he was desperately in need at the time and had told me to do whatever it took, and he needed to pay that bill. Based on me jogging his short-term memory he eventually paid. But he gave me a clue and real insight into his personality. I believed he was not a man of his word.

One day, John Calene, co-owner of Kornhauser and Calene and the head of the creative department, and I were walking back from a Spectravideo meeting, one of the very rare times we were alone on probably a ten-minute walk to our offices. John was a unique guy, very aloof and rarely had any use for account management people, as clearly his genius and interest was on the creative side.

He was saying something about Harry Fox, the Spectravideo president, and I told him I thought the Spectravideo president was mismanaging the company. I speculated there were shenanigans going on based on his behavior and, in my opinion, his mismanagement of the company and what I perceived were his "way too many" trips to China. I warned Calene we needed to be very careful with this company and make sure we didn't get stiffed on our bills. Even after raising over $6 million in a public stock offering, only seven months later Spectravideo was not paying our bills, demands for its products sank, and its stock went down from over six dollars a share down to 75 cents.

Obviously after that, Calene thought I was a genius. He took a liking to me as well because I had spoken the truth, I looked for an opportunity to talk to him, and tried to relate to him on his level, when most people would have run away or been scared to speak with him in the first place.

That's the key. You must be able to read people. Before you interact with people, you want to read them to the best of your ability, understand them, and respond accordingly. Also it doesn't hurt to have good insight and being right really helps... Smile!

TAKE ACTION

• Be willing to take chances to get things done. David Sanborn and Todrick Hall took time to meet with my kids simply because I asked them. These people are at the very top of their professions, but they responded to a simple, respectful request.

• What is one challenge you are facing, or task you have to do? Think outside the box and do whatever it takes to get the job done.

• You'll have impact by getting things done. And you'll get things done by knocking on lots of doors, making lots of phone calls, sending lots of e-mail, and asking for things.

• Become a student of people. Develop your people reading skills. Being able to read moods and intents will be very helpful to you—in life and in business.

CHAPTER 14

*T*AKE TIME TO UNDERSTAND PEOPLE

SNAPSHOT

1. Discover the value of understanding people where they are.

2. Understand the importance of getting people to "buy in."

3. Learn why sometimes you must be tough or toe the line no matter whose feelings get hurt.

The apostle Paul, a disciple of Jesus Christ, said, "I have become all things to all men, so I can get the message of Christ across." Paul knew one style wasn't going to do it for everybody. He had to relate to people where they were in order to get his message across. The same thing happens with us. We want to be impact players.

One time I was managing a TV production company in Florida and was a minority owner. I owned twenty percent of this company, and I had built the company from doing zero business to doing two million dollars a year in revenue with twenty-five employees. I had one particular employee, a veteran guy who was already working there when I took over the company. It was April, and the next day was opening day for the Florida Marlins baseball team. This employee told me he would be taking the next day off to go to the ballgame on opening day.

I looked at him and said, "No Bill, you can't do that. You can't just arbitrarily take a day off work without giving me sufficient advanced notice because you want to go to a ballgame. We have a business to run here. This is important. You need to be at work." He looked at me and said, "But it's opening day," as if I was crazy, and, of course, he could go.

I had to lay down the law in front of him and in front of the other sales people and employees of the company that no it wasn't okay for him to attend the ballgame. We were paying them to do a specific job, and do it when we expected them to do it. It wasn't just something they could do when it was convenient and not when they didn't feel like it or if something better came up. This guy was crushed, and he was upset with me. I told him if he went, he was fired.

I felt bad that I had to do this to the guy. I certainly didn't really mind if he went to a baseball game, but I had a point to prove to him and to the rest of the company, and I had to take a stand. So, he was furious with me. He didn't go to opening day, and he came in that day, as you could imagine, with a sour face and was furious.

At the end of the week I called him privately to my office and I said, "Bill, listen, I'm sorry you couldn't go to opening day, but you know what, I believe you were irresponsible in your thinking that it just didn't matter. I don't agree with your thinking. However, that said, I want to bless you. I've gotten you box seat tickets behind the dugout for a game over the weekend, and I have a limo taking you and your son down to the game. Enjoy the day. It's on me." He was so happy and loved it so much.

When I said he couldn't go to opening day, I was taking into account his feelings as well, but I had to stand up for my point. If I didn't stand up and take control over that room, in that company, with those people right then, they would have walked all over me. So, when it's time to be tough, you be tough. When it's time to be kind, you be kind. We want to motivate people.

I didn't want to lose him as an employee and have an enemy for life, so I figured out a way to get him back in my corner, stronger than ever. Remember, leadership and management are not about barking orders. It's about getting people to buy in. It's about purpose and passion— two things we've talked about.

On September 11, 2001 this country rallied together in unity after a terrorist attack, which included the destruction of the world trade towers in New York City.

Hey, sports teams rally and people rally around causes, like finding a cure for children who are sick, an election, or hurricane cleanup. People get inspired by circumstances, events, and other people. The key to being a good leader and a good manager is to understand people. Find out what makes them tick and operate accordingly. It's the same thing when you're getting ahead in your career, whether you want to be a manager or not, you need to understand people.

TAKE ACTION

• Sometimes you need to be tough, and sometimes you need to be soft. Knowing which time is which is crucial. Is there somewhere you need to be tougher? Somewhere you need to rebuild a bridge? Identify those spots, and then go for it!

• In business, and in life, finding out what makes people tick—what drives them—is a key to good relationships and success. Take the time to understand people. What makes your boss tick? Your key employees? Your spouse? Your kids? If you know that, you can act on it in a way that benefits everyone.

CHAPTER 15

SEEK GOOD COUNSEL

```
┌─────────────────────────────────────────────────────┐
│                     SNAPSHOT                          │
│ 1. Discover the value of seeking good counsel/advice  │
│ in areas where you need a little help.                │
│                                                       │
│ 2. Realize the power of learning from experience.     │
│                                                       │
│ 3. Understand the importance of matching your talents │
│ and abilities with the right industry or career for   │
│ you and why your inspiration and motivation is        │
│ critical.                                             │
└─────────────────────────────────────────────────────┘
```

One time I was facing some personal issues in life, a little unsure of my future, and I did something to motivate myself to break through, to achieve greatness, to live a life that matters, and to be an impact player. I sought some advice for the personal issue.

Now, I have gone to counselors before when appropriate—sometimes friends or even therapists. I strongly recommend that in life. Do not have this ego that you can't be trained, or that it is a weakness if you get help in a certain area. If I'm sick and have a cold or the flu, I want the doctor to give me medicine. If I break my back, I want the surgeon to fix me. So, if I have an emotional issue, I want to talk to somebody about it. If I have a spiritual issue I want to talk to somebody about it. Why? I want to get help. I want these fixed. I want to be running at my best potential all of my life—my mind, body, spirit. I want to operate at my peak efficiency for maximum results.

Many years ago, and I tell you this almost humorously, I said, "Look, imagine if I was sitting with Donald Trump (before he was elected president—I was just looking for his business insight), Benjamin Franklin, Bob Dylan and my father Jerry Levine, and I presented them with my situation."

Now a reminder this only happened in my mind. In the past I have sought counseling and advice from real people... Smile! Only this one time, I kind of envisioned in my mind what these people would say. I knew a lot about Donald Trump, I knew a lot about Bob Dylan, I knew a lot about Benjamin Franklin and, of course, I knew a lot about my father. So, I just imagined I was sitting there with them and I said, "Here is my problem. I'm a little concerned about the future—what the next business is going to be. It's not coming as quickly as I would like. I've had tremendous successes in the past but I really don't know what's next, and it's kind of bothering me a little bit. What should I do?"

I imagined Donald Trump sitting there, and I imagined him saying to me, "You're being an idiot! You've been tremendously successful. Look at me. I've had failures, but I learned from them. Not every deal works. Make new deals. It's not about what you want to do. It's about what you need to do." Wow, Donald, that's some pretty solid advice. Thanks.

My dad said the same thing to me, or at least in my mind this time, that he said to me many years ago. "It only takes one guy to say yes. Get back in the game. It's not over." Thanks, Dad.

Then Bob Dylan said, "Your life is your own. Why would you let others take it or judge it and live by their rules? Don't be imprisoned by the thoughts and will of others. Trust yourself to know what truly makes you happy."

I have listened to a lot of Bob Dylan's songs, and that's how I imagined Bob would have answered my question.

I've never met or talked to Ben Franklin. I've obviously never heard him on TV, but I've read many books about him. I imagined he would say, "You're being your own worst enemy. You only fail when you stop trying. A fool measures his own failures. Why would you stop playing when there's still innings left in the game, cards to be dealt, races to be run? A man who is his own judge, jury and prosecutor never wins a case. The future has yet to be lived. Why would you view it as history?" Wow! Thanks, Ben.

I'll tell you what, that little session with those guys got me refocused and back to the tasks at hand, more enthusiastic than ever.

So, why do I share this with you? Because it's imperative to get help and advice along the way. We're not perfect. We need coaching. We need help. We need advice. Remember, in any component of our lives—spiritual, physical, financial, emotional, relational—if we need guidance or help, we should reach out and ask for it. There is nothing wrong with doing that in a confidential manner.

When I wanted to learn about harness racing, I viewed it as a challenging hobby. I went to people who knew what they were doing, who had been in the industry, and who would teach me. I did the same thing when I wanted to learn about playing professional jai alai. I couldn't even get the ball out of the glove (it's called a cesta) the first time I tried. I had to learn and be shown, but when somebody taught me, and I practiced, I was able to do it and play at a professional level.

I tell you what, desperation is a great motivator. I have found that I have accomplished the greatest things in my life when I was desperate, scared, and had to do it. I found that comfort is the worst motivator and believe me, I enjoy being comfortable. I like doing what I want. Remember, I told you that money is freedom. It gives me the opportunity to do what I want and not be forced to do things. I like that, but I found I accomplish a lot less when I'm comfortable, and I accomplish a lot more when I'm desperate and motivated.

Inspiration is a great motivator, and going for what you want in life is a great motivator. Living your dream is a great motivator, and you should do all of those things. But remember one thing—you need to enjoy the ride. You need to enjoy yourself along the way. Of course it's hard work. Remember what Mr. Bewkes told me in the beginning. There was no shortcut, and once I found that out, I was willing to do whatever it took to get the job done—to get what I wanted.

I didn't mind that it was hard work, but you don't wait for the end to enjoy the reward. You enjoy your life as you're living it. That doesn't mean you don't have tough days, tough weeks, and times you're tired and bleary-eyed from working so hard and pushing yourself. Of course, you do.

Think of that athlete in the Super Bowl. The game starts, and a fan yells at him or his wife calls. He doesn't break from the huddle and tell the other guys, "Hey, guys, I've got to go take this call from my wife. I'll come back later." He doesn't go listen to the fan and answer the fan. No, he stays in the huddle and calls the play. Why? Because he's focused on the task at hand. He's prepared for this game. He's ready for it. He's trained for it. It's been his goal all his life and he's not going to get distracted.

Later, after he wins, he may be out celebrating with a steak dinner and partying with his buddies. That's great when it's time for that, but when the game was to be played, when the task was to be accomplished, he was focused one hundred percent on the task at hand. That is the key to success—focus, determination, inspiration and a willingness to do whatever it takes.

Tom Brady, in the super bowl in 2017, was losing badly in the third quarter, down by twenty-five points with three minutes to go. It looked like the game was over. He had played a terrible game, and he looked like he was going to be remembered as having failed/choked in a huge game. Did he quit? Did he stop? Did he give up? Nope. He and his team, they kept going, one play at a time, and they won the game in one of the greatest comebacks in sports history. That's our lives. Our concept for living should be the same!

I don't care if you win the race by being ahead every step of the way, or if you win the race after you were back thirty lengths the whole race until the last sixteenth of a mile and won in a photo-finish by a head or by a nose. You still won. That's all that matters, who won the race. It doesn't matter what position you were in during the middle of the race. It matters who won the race. You want to be that winner in life, and I know you will be.

So, it's important that you're not burdened by troubles, worries, cares and the weights of this world. By the way, you'll have all those things. You will have pressure. You'll have relationship pressure, financial pressure, physical pressure, emotional pressure, and spiritual pressure at one time or another, but you need to know how to control that. It's part of the game.

It's like the running back in football, who trains his body hard to be a running back. Then he goes and runs a play, and the other team hits him and tries to tackle him. He doesn't come back to the coach crying on the sidelines and saying, "I can't believe this. I can't believe the other team hit me." No, he knew they were going to hit him. He was prepared to be hit. He trained to be hit. This is what he lives for, and his goal was to break through them and get into the end zone to score a touchdown.

So, it shouldn't come as a surprise to you that there will be obstacles. There will be people against you, and sometimes your own heart and mind might be tired and might want to give up. Your body might be against you, but you have to keep going. You have to stay focused on the task at hand. You have to deal with those obstacles, burdens, and weights as if they are part of the game. They are!

When I'm driving to pick my son up from school, of course, I'd rather it not be pouring rain. I would like sunshine. But I'm still driving to get him, whether it's raining or not. Why? Because he's my son. I'm not leaving him stranded at school, even though I prefer it be one way. Whatever way it is, I am accomplishing the task at hand. You need to have that same attitude about your life and about your business. But please make sure to enjoy the ride along the way. You deserve that. That is a critical part of it.

I remember the story about a stockbroker, who was a very motivated guy, motivated to succeed. If anybody in the office wanted to come in and talk to him, they had to put a twenty-dollar bill in a fish bowl on his office desk. Why? Because he valued his time. He didn't want to talk about sports. He didn't want to talk about girlfriends, dinners, or Broadway shows. He wanted to focus on the task at hand when he was in that office, and if you were going to distract him, if you were going to take his time, you had to pay for it. Your attitude should be the same— focused, determined, single-minded on the task at hand.

I'm blessed to have many business skills. Among them are negotiating skills, sales ability, the ability to read people and a willingness to do what it takes to get the job done. But let me tell you something. A lot of these are learned skills. I've learned how to negotiate. It's an art form. I studied negotiation and practiced to get good at it. Now people look at me and tell me I'm an amazing negotiator. People call me up to help them negotiate their deals, and yes, I'm good at it. But you could do the same thing yourself. I just chose to learn it, as an art form and science, and continue to study it.

It's like a chess match. There are techniques, moves you make, things you do, depending on the situation and circumstances—like becoming a good driver. You learn how to drive in wet conditions, snowy conditions, windy conditions, and sunny conditions. You're going to learn how to drive on the highways when going seventy miles an hour and on a one lane country road going twenty miles an hour. Going over speed bumps and merging into traffic, it's all part of the learning process.

The same is true for sales and business. Yes, some people may have a more outgoing nature and some people have more talent and ability in certain areas. That's for sure. But these things are still skills that can be learned, just like the ability to read people and learn about timing and judging people. These are learned skills.

However, the willingness to do what it takes is a decision you have to make. It has to come from inside you. I can't teach you that. I can tell you that you need to do it, whether you have that desire already in you as a natural part of you or whether you have to make a conscious choice like you would if you were overweight, going into the gym and starting to lose weight. If you were failing a subject in school, you would go and get tutoring help as a conscious choice to make an effort to improve, to do what it takes and get the job done. That has to come from you.

Another important thing is you have to be adaptable. You have to be able to adjust to a situation. What do I mean? I want to give you one experience in my life that I hope you can relate to. As a young man, I always liked to write. I was a Bob Dylan and Bruce Springsteen fan, so I would write songs, and I learned how to play the guitar. I started to write a lot of original songs, but I had one major problem. I didn't sing very well, and I don't think the world was looking for another Bob Dylan. I thought I wrote great lyrics and I loved to sing and play the guitar. But I just couldn't carry a tune very well, and I realized I was not a musical creative genius.

So what did I do? Should I have gone on and pursued a career as a singer and songwriter? I realized there was a part of the talent for it that I didn't have. There was an element I needed. Again, I give an example of a five-foot four-inch basketball player looking to make it to the NBA. Probably not going to happen, even though you may have some of the skills, you don't have everything you need.

I knew I loved to write songs, and to this day I've never stopped writing. Occasionally, I still take out my guitar and sing as loudly as I can some of my original songs. However, rest assured, there is no one else in the house at the time, and I do that because it gives me pleasure and enjoyment. I went to college as a journalism major. I love to write. I really wanted to be a journalist. I was fascinated by it and it was a passion of mine I was looking forward to pursuing it as a career.

However, an interesting thing happened to me when I got to Syracuse University to the Newhouse School of Public Communications, one of the top journalism schools in the country. I was getting C's on some of my assignments and stuff I was handing in and even one time a D.

I thought, what's going on here? I'm writing this great stuff. I asked the professors why was I getting such crappy grades? How dare they give me C's and D's? And they looked at me and said, "Oh, your concepts are wonderful, but your grammar and punctuation is terrible, and, therefore, you're getting C's and D's." I said, "Wait a minute. Who cares about grammar and punctuation? That's why there are editors. My job is to come up with ideas and concepts. I'm not worried about where the commas and semi-colons go and specific punctuation and a perfection of the English language. I'm concerned with getting across concepts and ideas."

And they said, "Well, we do care about commas and punctuation, and you're getting C's and D's." So what did I do? I immediately went into advertising. Where concepts and ideas mattered but punctuation and grammar didn't. I took my career down that path and was blessed very much with a career in advertising, which led to TV production, which led to marketing, which led to other businesses and entrepreneurial stuff—real estate development, renewable energy, manufacturing, specialty food distribution, publishing, and a host of other industries I got involved in.

I adjusted accordingly to the situation at hand. I maximized my skills where they could bring me the best return. Oh, I still wanted to be a singer on stage, like Bob Dylan, and I also wanted to be a baseball player for the Yankees when I grew up. I didn't have the ability and the opportunity to do that, but I still play baseball all the time.

I get to play baseball, and I get to play my guitar. I just don't do it on a national stage in front of thousands of screaming fans and I don't get paid to do it. But I still love and enjoy it. I used my professional skills where I could get paid, where they were most efficient and effective, and I could maximize them. I adjusted accordingly.

Even in journalism, I didn't say, "Oh well. I'm going to make myself miserable worrying about punctuation." No. I'm sure those are very valid points the professors were making from their perspective, but from my perspective, it was about the idea and the concept. So I found an arena, advertising, that allowed my talent to explode and me to use it freely. Then I loved what I was doing. It allowed me to use my business skills, my marketing skills, my writing, everything.

But I had to be motivated and I had to be open-minded. I had to be looking for a better fit. I had to be smart. I had to not be so stuck on one thing that I couldn't see another opportunity in front of me, and that's the point I'm making to you. Had I been determined to be a singer no matter what, I would have had a pretty crappy life. Had I been determined to be a journalist no matter what, I would have had a pretty crappy life.

Ironically enough, I went on to become a writer. I've written many books on some of my favorite topics—God, business, motivational topics and overcoming addiction. Why? Because I believe you or I should be able to speak intelligently on topics that we have passion about and knowledge about—either through personal experience or that we've learned about.

How funny is that? The kid they would give C's and D's to in journalism class for grammar and punctuation is writing books. Now, of course, I have editors who help me with punctuation because, truthfully, I don't want to look like an idiot if I don't have to. But when I write, I write exactly as I feel. I don't worry about punctuation or grammar or anything. I speak and write what I'm feeling and thinking.

Then I give it to a professional editor to correct and place commas, colons, and periods in their proper places and suggest I split up a long sentence or tell me to check a factual reference I've made. That's fine... but I don't ever let them change my voice. I had an editor on my first book, *Don't Blow It with God*, and she was changing every word. I would say cop, and she would say policeman. I would say maid and she would say house servant. I said, "Hey, you can't do this. You can't change my voice and change the way I'm speaking and what I'm saying. You can fix punctuation, but you can't change what I say or how I say it." So, I fired her and found other editors to work with who understood what I was trying to accomplish and helped me very much.

Remember, it's good to have help in areas where you're weak, especially when it's imperative in getting the job done. But the point I'm trying to make is, look, I owned up to it. I moved with it. I shifted with situations and opportunities as they came up and was able to use my skills accordingly instead of locking myself in a box or branding myself in a specific place emotionally, physically, mentally. Instead, I was open to the opportunity in front of me, and that has led me to some of the greatest opportunities in my life, things I had never seen coming— opportunities in business, real estate, development, investing in different businesses, in different people because I was willing to look at opportunities. I was willing to do things other people wouldn't do to get what I wanted. And to this day, I still do that same thing.

Just a note if there was not advertising to go into and I had to stay in journalism, I would have adapted, played by their rules, and done everything I could and succeeded to reach my goal... but I wouldn't have liked it.

TAKE⚡ACTION

• Make sure to get advice from people—both living and dead! What would that important person in your life have said about what you're planning to do? Running these sorts of conversations, even in your own mind, can bring great clarity.

• Are you currently burdened by persistent relationship, financial, physical, emotional or spiritual pressures? Think about where you might seek good counsel. This will help you stay focused and move forward on the path to success.

• If you could ask any three people (living or dead) for advice... who would they be and what do you think they would say to you?

• You have to decide what's important to you and what you're willing to do to achieve your goals. Nobody else can do that for you—and if you aren't honest with yourself, you'll fall way short.

• It's good to be adaptable, but don't try to fit a square peg into a round hole. If you're in a situation where you're the square peg, nobody—including you—will benefit from trying to force a fit.

• Are you truly willing to do whatever it takes to succeed within legal and ethical boundaries? Remember, this has to come from within you; someone else cannot give you this desire.

CHAPTER 16

Do it the Right Way

> ### SNAPSHOT
> 1. Learn why it is vitally important to walk in integrity in your business.
>
> 2. Discover why you need to operate in clarity and objectivity before choosing your next business partner.
>
> 3. Understand why doing the right thing eventually pays off on the path to success.

I had a partner in my first TV Production company (the one where I wouldn't let the guy go to the baseball game). I owned twenty percent; he owned eighty percent. He funded the business, and my job was to run it and operate it. I learned a very important lesson in the years we worked together. I built a business from scratch, and we were well on our way to becoming an extremely successful company. I was excited. I had twenty percent of the company.

I thought the stock was going to make me millions of dollars. We had plans to take that particular company public, but I, unfortunately, had made a mistake in judgment. I had known the guy who owned the other eighty percent of the company from working together in another industry and becoming friends. He was a great guy and took care of me. He helped me when I needed help. I had back surgery years prior, and he helped me tremendously during my surgery and recovery. He covered for me in the business and he was really a great friend.

However, he never treated other people very well. He was very spoiled, having grown up very rich and entitled, and he looked down on people. He was not a man of his word and lied to a lot of people. Many thought he was stuck up and arrogant, but I just looked at him only based on the way he treated me. I watched him treat other people badly and not keep his word, but I thought since he had treated me well in the past, I would just judge him and look at him based on the way he was treating me. I admit now, not proudly, that was a convenient and self-serving way to think.

Well, I learned a lesson from that experience. As it turned out, his personality was to be demeaning to people, to not care about them, to not keep his word, in essence, to rip them off when he thought it was in his advantage to do so. Even though he hadn't yet done that to me, he did it to other people.

Eventually, he did do it to me. Two years into the business, he was having an affair with one of the secretaries, and he was stealing money. I don't understand why you have to steal money when you own eighty percent of a company. You can have eighty percent of it anyway. He was irrational in his treatment of his employees and how he made his decisions. He was doing stuff to hurt the company dramatically, and God taught me a lesson.

By the way, if you don't believe in God you can and should still learn the lesson and apply it to yourself. It is on a personal note I just share with you that I believe the wisdom came to me from God. He showed me the light and the taught me a lesson and that was you can't be half clean. In other words, I always knew this guy was not true to his word, but I was willing to overlook it based on the way he treated me.

I learned you can't be half clean. It's one thing if you don't know something and find out later. You can't be held responsible. But if you did know it, you shouldn't be surprised. You know that example of who is more guilty, the guy who knew the speed limit was fifty-five and was going ninety or the guy who didn't know there was a speed limit? Clearly, the one who knew was guiltier.

God just revealed to me that he wasn't going to let me have success if I did the wrong thing, if I wasn't a man of integrity, or if I aligned myself with people who were not doing the right things. You may prosper for a little while. It may look good for a bit, but I assure you in the end, it will not work out.

The Bible has a verse that says there is a way that seems right to a man, but in the end, it leads to death. In this book, I'm not speaking to you about God or religion. That's your own private decision. I'm here to speak to you about business and leadership, but I give you that parable because it's an excellent depiction of business and life.

I believe you need to be a man of integrity. One of the things my father taught me as a young man and always instilled in me is that a man is only as good as his word. If I do something, if I say something, I am to do it. If I made a bad deal, I have to live with it. If a made a good deal, good for me. But my word needs to be my bond, and people need to be able to count on my word. That was probably some of the best advice I ever got.

I had to leave that company where the guy who owned eighty percent was ripping me off. I left with nothing in order to get out of there and start the next company, which fortunately was extremely successful. I started that with a partner I shared the same core values with, who was a good man and did the right thing. We ran our TV production company joyfully and productively for almost a decade and built it up. I sold that company to pursue ministry and charity work and other entrepreneurial adventures, and life has continued to be a very exciting and wonderful ride since then.

The bottom line is you need to be involved with people who are doing the right thing, and it will pay off. I see many people in business who have looked for an advantage, who have looked to have great gain, who have made great gains, and have given it all back and wound up in jail cells, broke and/or disgraced because they did things the wrong way.

Believe me, they might have been riding high for a little while, but they didn't think it was worth it in the end. You don't want to be that guy. You want to do things the right way. I remember sitting with Erwin McManus, a nationally known and much loved pastor and author, one day talking about people and business. He looked at me over dinner and said, "I don't understand it. I don't understand why people just can't do good. There is so much money to be made in the world by just doing good things and helping people, why wouldn't people just do good?"

And I thought, "Man, he's right. Why do people think about ways to do evil things and wrong things and take advantage of people?" I guess I would almost understand that if it was the only option to succeed. But it's not.

There is so much opportunity to make money and to do good things and help people. That should be the attitude of our hearts, and I believe we would be blessed by that. Then at least the money we make we'll be keeping. No one will be looking to take it from us.

TAKE ACTION

- Ultimately, your integrity is all you have. Guard it with your life! It is that valuable.

- The people you are associating with can hurt you either personally or professionally.

- Decide if you agree with what Erwin McManus said to me, "There is so much opportunity to make money and to do good things and help people." I believe that should be our attitude!

- What are some areas where you are tempted to do something you know is wrong to achieve the result you want? Stop doing it. Trust me—in the long run, those ethical shortcuts will destroy you.

- Someone who cuts moral corners in one area will almost certainly do it in other areas. Why should your boss trust you if your spouse can't? Why should your children trust you if your employees can't? Make it a goal to be someone who does what you say and means what you say.

CHAPTER 17

BUILD A SMART TEAM

SNAPSHOT

1. Discover why you should align your thinking and actions with your stated mission.

2. Understand the importance of surrounding yourself with a smart team of people who are well-motivated.

3. Learn to focus and prioritize what is important to maximize your time and effort.

I had a particular boss at NW Ayer Advertising named Lamar LeMonte. Lamar was one of my favorite bosses early on. He was so smooth and cool, and he was well respected in the agency, but he was sly as a fox. One interesting thing about Lamar is that, at the end of every day, nothing was left on his desk. He put everything away and started every day with a clean desk.

He was a hard worker, a management supervisor for the AT&T account, and he got a lot done and he was also able to motivate employees. Most importantly, he knew how to climb the corporate ladder. Lamar was a great boss, and he was encouraging. I was able to learn a lot from watching him. One day he came up to me apologetically and said, "I need you to do me a favor. I am sorry to ask you this. I know you're an assistant account executive and not an errand boy, but I have to go to this meeting, and I need you to pick up my dry cleaning. My time is more valuable than yours." And he handed me his dry-cleaning receipt! Lamar wasn't being mean. He was just being realistic and gave me a good dose of reality. His time was more valuable.

That inspired me. I was determined to get to the point in my life and career where my time was more valuable than other people's. I really admired Lamar for the way he navigated the political and personal landscape of the company in order to further his own career, whether it was creating strategic friendships and relationships, analyzing the agency's needs to further his career, cozying up to the bosses, performing professionally at a top level, or managing and motivating people.

He knew what he wanted, he was motivated, and he knew how to get it. I admired that. Many business people will tell you, and this is probably the greatest lesson you can learn, you need to surround yourself with people smarter than you. Hey, it's nice for the ego to be the smartest person at the table and have everybody seeking your opinion. And of course, you can be that way by simply just being the boss and ramming your opinion and thoughts and dictates onto people, but that's not the best way to get ahead.

The best way to get ahead is by surrounding yourself with people who are smarter than you, who can help you get to where you're going. On that note, if you want good people, you need to be able to pay them well, so as to motivate them with financial reward, professional gain and personal satisfaction. Underpaying people is one way to make them miserable quickly and is not a good idea, especially if you can afford to do otherwise.

Of course, in the beginning of a company, when money is tight, people understand that, as long as they are tied in to an equity or bonus situation. If they believe the future will get better, they will do anything for you if they believe in you. This is not a unique concept. It is just a factual one and one you need to take to heart.

You need people who are thinkers, who will come up with ideas, and then people to implement and execute them. Just remember, if you already knew everything to do, you would be doing it. There's no embarrassment or shame to not be the smartest guy in the room. It's quite a talent to be able to organize, manage, inspire, influence, encourage and motivate talent to get the best out of them so that the team and organization succeeds. That is what an owner or manager is supposed to do. I don't have to be the best at everything. Of course, I should know everything, know every job in the industry, and know my company well, but I don't have to be the best in everything.

My definition of a genius is one who is able to delegate, inspire and find others who can contribute to his cause and company to make it progress, grow and explode quicker. That leads to financial rewards and a much happier, less stressful life. Today, with the internet, it is easy to access good talent physically, virtually and digitally, so there is no excuse for not working with talented, good people.

I remember going to a conference and hearing Marcus Buckingham speak. I did not know who he was before I heard him speak, but later I found out he was an author, motivator and business consultant. The one thing that stuck out to me most when he spoke was this particular line. He said, "Do what's most important now."

He talked about your to-do list, obligations, and people seeing the large list of things they have to do. Most people do the six things that are easiest because you can get them off the list quickly. He said that was stupid because it was distracting and not the way to run your life or business.

He's said you have to do what's most important now, not what's easiest. I adopted that strategy many years ago and found it to be a tremendous blessing. Of course, I keep lists of things that need to be done. You can do it on paper, on your computer, or on your phone, but I learned long ago this list is not my enemy. It's not meant to hurt me or defeat me. Quite the opposite, the list is my friend. It's a guide and tells me where I need to go and when I need to go there, but it does not rule my life. I'm not ruined or destroyed or upset if the list doesn't get accomplished because I learned long ago I can never beat the list. I can never make it go away. I'll never be finished. That's when I realized the list was my friend. It was there to guide me, assist me, and help put me in the right direction on a daily basis.

Marcus Buckingham's advice, while not original, was communicated very well, and I want to pass on to you. Do what's most important now. Stay focused on the task at hand. Doing that will advance your business, mission, and purpose forward. Do not get distracted by little details and things that take up your time but are not accomplishing your goal.

It's a very simple theory. Many people refer to it as a mission statement these days. Having a mission statement is irrelevant if you don't live it. What do I mean? If you have a mission statement, every action you take, everything you do is supposed to go toward accomplishing your mission statement. If it's not accomplishing your mission statement, don't do it. That's how you know whether something is valuable to you or not.

For instance, if our mission statement is to make the greatest hamburger in the world and serve it to our customers, everything we're doing in our day should be contributing to that mission statement. If it's not, we shouldn't do it. You can have both personal and professional mission statements. They are a great way to stay focused. Some people have rallying cries, taglines, or theme lines in their organization that they try to live up to every day. That's how they manage their time. They measure their actions against their goals and make sure their actions are accomplishing their goals. Otherwise they don't take that particular action. That is an extremely effective way of thinking, acting and behaving to accomplish your goal and mission.

My mission statement is: Make a positive impact in the lives of others by sharing the knowledge I have to motivate and inspire people to be happier and enjoy life.

TAKE ACTION

• If you surround yourself with people smarter than you are, they will make you better and more successful. Who are some good, smart people you need to align yourself with?

• Successful people find people who can contribute to the task at hand. They then inspire them and delegate to them. What people do you know who have the tools to help you accomplish your goals? Enlist them!

• Do what's most important now. Prioritizing correctly can be the difference between success and failure. What really needs to be done now, and what just wants to be done right now? Figure out the difference, and do the thing that needs to be done right now.

• Write your own mission statement. Boil it down to what truly motivates you and what you want to accomplish. Then use it to set your priorities. For every task that comes to you, ask yourself, "Does this best help me accomplish my mission?" If not, don't do it! At least not yet. Do the thing that will move your mission forward.

CHAPTER 18

OVERCOMING HIDDEN OBJECTIONS

SNAPSHOT
1. Learn the key objections you will need to overcome in life and business.

2. Discover the importance of communicating why you do what you do.

3. Understand the importance of learning from history.

In business and life sometimes there are hidden objections, things people are thinking that they might not necessarily tell you or ask you. These can dramatically affect—good or bad—how you build credibility in your business and how you get ahead. Here are some lessons I've learned.

Lesson 1. The first thing people think, "Can I trust you?

"Why should I believe you? Prove it." Well, one way I can tell if I can trust somebody is to check out their past. Rest assured everybody is checking out yours. People check references through the internet. They will definitely Google you, search out and find any other information available about you, including people who have previously done business with you, customers, coworkers, and former bosses.

If you can't be trusted, word will get around quickly. People may still do business with you, but they will know in their hearts and minds that they cannot trust you. It will come back to haunt you.

So, why should people believe you? They should believe you based on your past performance, based on what you've done, not based on what you say you're going to do. In that regard, you want to make sure you have done what you've said over time and that you are a person people can depend on, count on, and trust. You can't put a price on that. It is one of the most valuable tools you can have in the business world today.

You can't advertise or announce that you're trustworthy, you have to prove it through past performance! People will know and come to see it very quickly. It will impact your success greatly.

Lesson 2. Don't screw me.

People don't want to be screwed. They don't want to be ripped off. They don't want to be burned or taken advantage of. In other words, you have to be good to your word. You have to treat people as you want to be treated or better. You have to go out of your way to make sure your customer or client is satisfied. You have to put his interest ahead of your own and truly do a great job. This applies to all business and relationships.

As an ad agency, that was so important to us. We worked hard to learn our clients' businesses as well or better than they knew them so we could produce the best advertising possible. This strategy created results, increased sales and increased performance for the company. We truly considered ourselves partners with the companies we worked with.

Most importantly, people want to know you're not going to screw them. An employer wants to know you're not going to steal from him. You're not going to recruit his employees. You're not going to take his clients. You're not going to look to open up your own business to compete with him. Basically, you're going to do the right thing. Your clients and customers want to know the same thing—that you're not going to take advantage of them. You're not going to rip them off. You're going to do the right thing and act in their best interest.

Imagine if you had a lawyer who didn't care if he won your case. He didn't prepare accordingly. Imagine if you had a doctor who didn't care If he saved your life, so he was not prepared for your surgery. He just wanted your money and his fee. You would be aghast. You would say, "I can't believe we put this trust in you and you let us down. We gave you this trust. You were supposed to be above reproach." That's right and it's the same with you and me in business.

Lesson 3. Why did you do that?

People want to know why you did things. Your employees want to know why you have a certain strategy, and why you are implementing certain procedures and policies. Why are we doing what we're doing? They want to know so they can buy in, be on your side, and work even harder. You want them to know that and to buy in. So, it's not enough to tell people what to do. We have to get them to buy in.

We have to explain to them why, and it has to make sense. When people know why you're doing things, they will respond quite differently. For instance, if you are driving your car on the highway, and you are cut off by a car who almost causes an accident, weaving in and out of traffic and cutting you off, you're thinking, that stupid jerk. I can't believe this guy's driving. He almost killed me. What an idiot. He belongs in jail.

However, if you pulled up later and found that the guy's baby was dying in the back seat of the car, and he was rushing the baby to the hospital to save his life, instead of being upset with the guy and mad, you would now completely understand why he did what he did. Not only would you no longer be mad, but you would rush ahead to give him an escort and cut off traffic for him. That's right. The exact same circumstance, the exact same situation but a different reaction based on your perception of why he did what he did. It's critical that people understand why you do what you do.

Lesson 4. Could it be better?

We need to constantly evaluate what we do and how we do it. Did we miss the mark? Did we go astray? In golf, if you miss the cup by an inch, you still missed. So, we constantly want to evaluate ourselves, even when we think we're at our best. We constantly want to see how we can make things better.

We constantly want to probe people for ideas of how things can be better. What can we fix? What can we improve? This is a strategy the Walt Disney Company uses very well, and many other companies have employed very well—constant self-evaluation. While one part of the company may be delighted and excited with the job they did and the excellence they've achieved, another part of the company is constantly looking to redefine, make better, examine and improve every single aspect of the company. It could be company service, sales, shipping, production, manufacturing, customer relations, management styles, etc. It doesn't matter. The concept applies to every aspect of every area of your business.

So, you should constantly be asking, could it be better? Rest assured, your competition is thinking the same thing and plenty of smart people will stay ahead of the game and ahead of you if you don't keep improving. Again, look at the folks at Polaroid, Eastman Kodak, Blockbuster Video and many other companies that are now obsolete because they did not stay abreast of technology and changing times. They did not look to improve their product and make it better, thinking they could rest on reputation and past performance. That does not work in the business world. Keep innovating.

Lesson 5. You don't understand me.

Your employees, the people you work with, your clients, your vendors—everyone wants to feel understood and appreciated. And I agree that is not always possible as some people make it impossible by their behavior and attitude. But for the most part and for most people, this works well. People want to believe you understand them.

How do you understand somebody? You take time to understand them. You talk to them. You befriend them. You engage in relationships with them. You observe them, and you begin to understand what motivates them. What is important to them? Why do they do what they do? If you can understand that, you can motivate them much more efficiently and much better.

By the way, this is not to take advantage of people and control them. Quite the opposite, this is to motivate them and inspire them to accomplish the task at hand—

hopefully, the task you assigned them to do or the desired result you want to get. What do I mean? If I know a guy is working to send his kid to college, that helps me. He has a different motivation than the guy who is working to retire or the guy who doesn't really care if he's working or not but has a job anyway. Everyone's motivations are different.

If a guy is an ardent baseball fan, lives and dies for baseball, his motivations, likes and dislikes are different from someone who is an Oprah Winfrey talk show fan or loves to go fishing or bike riding. What if a guy is very political and everything he does or thinks revolves around who's in office and what the president, congress, and local politicians are doing? His mind works differently from a guy whose love is sports. And that mind thinks differently from a guy who may have been in love or a guy who's caring for a sick mother.

All these factors contribute to each person. It's a combination of factors, but with some observation, with some study, with some care, with some concern, with investment of some time, we can really find out what makes people tick. We can understand them, and they will not feel misunderstood. They will feel appreciated.

You might not agree with everything everybody thinks or does, but you'll understand it. And that's the point. I'm not asking you to be Mother Teresa. I'm not asking you to make your shoulder available for everybody to cry on. I'm not asking you to be a psychologist, a psychiatrist, or a therapist, but I am asking you to be an intelligent businessman who knows how to read people and under-stand people.

You want to be able to read what they're made of, what motivates them, and what inspires them. You can then respond accordingly to each person so you can get the maximum effort, participation and performance from each person. That's an investment you have to make personally so you have better people in your company who help your team and company grow faster and accomplish more.

Lesson 6. Did you learn from history?

Of course, you know the famous line, if you don't learn from history, you're destined to repeat it. I remember Bill Ackman, famous hedge fund manager, who brought in Ron Johnson, a former high-ranking executive at Apple, to run JC Penney Department Store after Ackman had just taken a large equity stake in the company.

Ackman had bragged that he was going to turn around JC Penney. He had three-hour presentations with pie charts about how he was going to maximize the floor space to get much more per square foot in revenue. Now, with Johnson coming in, they were going to triple what was done previously because Johnson was going to use his expertise from working with Apple all these years and making Apple one of the leading companies in the world. He was going to apply his magic to JC Penney, and the company and its stock was going to go through the roof.

Well, it only took fourteen months before Johnson was out the door. He was a complete failure and flopped. Not as a person, but as a businessman in this particular instance. Why? Because the things that worked for him at Apple did not translate into the JC Penney world. What worked in technology and computers didn't translate into retail. Johnson and Ackman both learned this the hard way. Throwing in the towel, taking a huge loss on his investment, Ackman sold his shares and later admitted that he had made a mistake in thinking Johnson's strategies and philosophies from Apple and technology would translate into the retail world. He didn't learn from history. We should learn from that!

It doesn't mean that Johnson couldn't have been a success, and Ackman is certainly no idiot although he has had his share of mistakes as well as successes. It means if I am handicapping a horse race and the horse has lost the last fifteen races in a row, and he's running in the same class on the same track today against the same quality of horse, it is very unlikely he would win the race today. Why? Because history shows he can't do it. Now, I guess if all the other horses fall down and break a leg, and he remains standing, he could win. But that is highly unlikely. So, we want to learn from history. Ackman had no basis except that he had made a conclusion in his own mind that this would work. But, he had no historical basis for that thinking.

That's just one example. Usually an employee who is trouble in one company is trouble in another. Maybe he was not truthful. He was not loyal to the company, he did underhanded things and used underhanded sales tactics or was a backbiter and not a team player. These characteristics rarely change. They could, obviously, if a guy has a spiritual awakening, a business awakening, or an incident in his life changes his attitude. I have seen remarkable changes in people. It could happen, but those are few and far between. For the most part, we know people by their actions. We know a dog by its tricks. We should be able to know the type of people we are dealing with.

I previously told you about my partner in the TV production company where I owned twenty percent of the company. I learned you can't be with people who are not men of integrity, and you cannot be half clean. So, we need to learn from history, and from people, from companies, from situations, from life, from business.

Remember we need to learn from history.

Our job is not to follow our competitors and do what they do. Although, when Papa John started Papa John's Pizza, his goal was to get five percent of Domino's business. That's all he wanted to do, and he'd consider it to be a success. Of course, he got much more than that!

In that case, copying an existing business was a good idea, and it can work in certain instances. Again, you need to know your market, your demographics, the volume being done in that market and what percent of market share you think you can get. However, in most cases, you need to think out of the box, uniquely.

TAKE ACTION

• What are the hidden objections people around me have to what I'm trying to accomplish? Identify those things, and then come up with a plan to disarm those objections.

• Let history be your guide. Have any people tried to do what you're trying to do? Has anyone faced the same obstacles to their goals that you're facing? If so, find out what they did and if it worked. Learn from them!

CHAPTER 19

THE MOST IMPORTANT LESSONS EVER

THE RECAP AND REVIEW

So let's review, here are the most important lessons I've learned in business:

1. Sometimes you have to motivate different people differently to get them to think the same.

The same techniques do not work on everybody. What do I mean? Well it's simple. One guy you may have to talk to softly, with encouragement telling him how great he is. Another guy you may have to hammer, tell him he's not good enough, and challenge him that way. Some guys are revolutionaries and some followers. Some are soft and some hard. As a manager, a motivator, and a leader of people, you need to be able to get people to accomplish the task at hand. People are different, and that's why, while the goal and mission is the same, sometimes you have to tell different people different things to get them to think the same. I believe communication is key. It can inspire, motivate, and invigorate or it can hurt, crush and destroy. It is a tool. In order for a tool to be effective, you must learn how to use it properly. Then you can use it how you want. I hope you will use it to have a positive impact on people and in life. I believe communication can fix or prevent a lot of problems and is a great tool to have.

2. You can't be half clean.

As I discussed, when I owned my first television production company with a partner who was not good to his word, it impacted me. Walk in full integrity in your business and with partners, clients, suppliers and everyone you deal with.

3. You need to do whatever it takes to get the job done.

I REPEAT… You need to do WHATEVER it takes to get the job done—of course while retaining your integrity and remaining legal, moral, and ethical!

4. People make you money.

I learned this no place better than in Hamilton County, Florida, when I got involved in real estate development. I invested time and effort in people and their loyalty. Those relationships made me money and got me access to deals that I never would have had if I had not invested time and effort into those people. They became friends as well, but the bottom line is people, connections, and relationships can make you a lot of money. You need to invest in people. That's where ingenuity, ideas and opportunity you may never know existed come from— loyalty, teamwork and a group effort to accomplish what's never been accomplished before. People make you money.

5. You can't put a price on integrity.

As my father also taught me, you must be good to your word. People may do business with a man who's not good to his word, but it's not because they want to. It's because they have to. They don't trust him and they know they're going to get screwed. When you are good to your word, people go out of their way to do things for you and to honor their word with you as well. On that same note, don't do business with people who are not good to their word. You will get screwed in the end and burned. It is just a question of when and how. That is a guarantee.

6. Quality sells.

I remember going to buy a television when I had just graduated college and my budget was $300. I was very determined that I was only going to spend $300 on this television. When I got to the store with a buddy of mine, we looked at the $300 televisions. They were cheap and not made very well. But that was okay. That was my budget and it was going to be a brand-new television, so I was happy.

My friend saw a $500 television and told me I should buy it. I said, "Are you kidding? I'm not spending that kind of money." He said, "This $300 television is going to break in a couple of years. This $500 television is going to last you all of your life. It is actually cheaper to purchase it if you do the math, breaking down the cost per year based on how long you're going to own it." Well, of course, he was right. If I amortized the cost of a $500 television that's going to last me twenty years, that comes out to $25 a year. If I amortize out the cost of a $300 television that's going to last me five years, it comes out to $60 a year. So clearly, the bargain was in the more expensive television.

It's the same when you invest in employees, products, machinery, and relationships. Quality sells. You can't hire a kid out of college for thirty thousand dollars and expect him to perform at the level of a hundred-and-fifty-thousand dollar seasoned executive. Now, of course, if you don't have the hundred and fifty thousand and only have the thirty thousand, clearly you have no choice. But sometimes we can be penny wise and dollar foolish. By trying to save pennies here and there, we never get the task accomplished and in essence everything we spent was wasted.

My son, Jackson, when he was ten years old wanted to buy this $200 Japanese Pokémon card holder that you could wear on your arm. The thing wrapped around your wrist and held five cards at the same time so you could see and play the Pokémon game. I said, "Jackson, this is a tremendous waste of money. You're spending $200 on a single toy. You have no concept or clue about money."

But it was money he had gotten as presents for birthdays and holidays. I thought, okay I'm going to teach him a lesson. I said, son, it's your money, if you want to spend it that way, you can spend it. And sure enough he bought the toy. It came overseas from Japan as he wanted only the original model made in Japan and not the knock-off one from America. And that toy wound up being a great deal. He got tremendous value for his money. Not only did he get a free t-shirt but the toy was amazing, it was well built and I had to admit to him that I stood corrected. That it was actually an astute investment. Remember, quality wins!

7. A reminder of some of the important lessons my dad taught me:

- "Trees don't grow to the sky. Nothing lasts forever."
- "A fool and his money are soon parted." Quoting W.C.Fields, and then Dad beautifully added… "and an idiot and his ass are soon broken."
- "Sleep on it… things always look different in the morning." This saying always reminds me that sometimes we get caught up in the excitement of things. We should always take a step back after the excitement has died down and take a levelheaded, clear look at what we were

so excited about. We need to pay attention to what we're doing and not get caught up in insanity or other people's garbage. You know the old story about the king who has no clothes (If not, look it up and read it). The old fable is a lesson to be well-learned by those who invested in tulips, the NASDAQ bubble, the housing bubble, many fake cures for cancer and other stuff. People talk a good game. Some people say money talks. Yes, but I say, "If money talks, than reality speaks!"

- "The boss sets the pace." You can't expect people to do something that you won't do yourself. If people see you working hard, they work hard.
- "You only need one person to say yes." Don't get discouraged by rejection. Keep going until you find someone to give you the opportunity, position, or ability to do or get what you want.
- "Keep your head about you when all others are losing theirs." Dad quoting Winston Churchill (who quoted Rudyard Kipling), a great and constant reminder from Dad to stay levelheaded and don't let emotions get the best of you.
- "Monday follows Sunday." This was Dad's beautiful perspective and wisdom in essence reminding me that life goes on no matter how tragic, insurmountable or life-changing things and events may seem. Somehow the world has a beautiful and distinct way of continuing to move forward and I should remember that and take a long-term perspective on life (and investing)!

8. If you want to control something, you need to own it.

That's a lesson I learned in publishing my books under Great Hope Publishing label. I didn't want to be edited. I didn't want to be told what to do, and the only way I could do that was to own it or control it myself.

9. Learn from the experts.

As I learned when I took up Jai Alai and harness racing and the same lesson goes in business—learn from the experts. You want to learn from people who know what they're doing. They can teach you quickly and efficiently. You want to learn from the best.

10. You need the right people in place.

The right people are worth everything. That goes back in with you get what you pay for. When promoting one book, I hired a company that had great expertise in one area but wasn't as proficient in other areas. I liked them very much. They tried hard, but they weren't the right fit for the job. I just took whoever was available and I thought they could do the job. That was a big mistake. I should have made sure they could do the job.

11. Do not be scared to go where no man has gone before.

Many of my businesses—renewable energy, land development, publishing, addiction rehabilitation and education, public speaking—were new opportunities for me, things I had never done before. But they all excited me, got me fired up, and I was willing to do whatever it took to learn about them. Had I simply stayed and labeled myself as an "advertising guy" all of my life, even though that was my college major and my early career, I would have never branched out into these other areas that not only brought me pleasure but money. That doesn't mean it's a bad thing to stay in one area. That's okay if it's your choice. But it also means there are other opportunities. You need to keep your eyes open to opportunity and not be scared to take the leap when you see one.

12. Align yourself with winners.

Better to get into business with a guy who is successful and take a little less of the company than to go into business with a guy who has failed five times and own more of it. Remember, I'd rather have three, five, ten, twenty, thirty percent of a successful company than one hundred percent or eighty percent of one that is a failure.

13. The older you get, the more balance you will need in your life.

Do everything you can while you're young. Work as hard as you can while you're young to get ahead of the game. Tell yourself to focus yourself singularly on the task at hand, until you have established a foundation that allows you to switch over your currency value from money to time because the older you get, time will become the more valuable currency. However, in order to have time to spend the way you want, you have to make money early. So do whatever it takes, but don't forget you'll need that balance later. Of course, many experts talk about other business lessons. Some say hard work will always outweigh talent. I'm not sure I agree with that. Hard work is a minimum requirement to get ahead. It is like having a college degree. It simply gets you in the game. A lot of people work hard but do not get ahead. Hard work is a key ingredient to getting ahead, but it is not the only ingredient. And it doesn't always outweigh talent.

14. Be confident enough to accept your faults.

Know who you are, be able to accept yourself as you are, and knowing where your weaknesses and strengths are. Play up your strengths and find somebody who can do the things you can't do well.

15. Learn from the past.

Clearly we'd agree with that one. If you don't learn from history, you're doomed to repeat it. Or, as we say in recovery, the definition of insanity is repeating the same behavior and expecting different results. Remember, there is always more you can do by continuing to learn. We never know it all. We can't stop learning. Just look at the folks at Polaroid, Blockbuster, Kodak and many other now extinct or defunct companies who refused to continue to learn. Yes, I know I've told you this three times, so you know its really important!

16. Don't be afraid to get started.

You've got to start somewhere. You've got to get that ball going. You can't hit that ball if you don't swing the bat. So while you may have big dreams, you need to start somewhere. I believe you need to be out among people. I believe motion begets motion, and action begets action. So don't spend your whole life thinking about something. Even if you don't know how it's going to turn out, start doing it and learn. That's how I learned on Madison Avenue. I got into the game. That's how you learn. You get started. You're going to fail. That's okay, babies fall before they learn to walk. You don't ride a bicycle perfectly the first time. We make mistakes in business, sports, and life. It's okay. We get back up. We learn from them and move forward. Remember it's not about perfection it's about progress!

17. Keep What You Earn.

When you do make a lot of money—and I know you will—there is very strategic stuff you should do to protect your assets, including estate planning and money management. That's another book and another subject but an important one to make sure you protect and keep what you worked so hard to earn. I could tell you stories of people who weren't so prudent and didn't seek advice and counsel on these things. Even though they didn't necessarily do anything wrong, somebody sued them or attacked them or they got caught up or involved in something and wound up suffering tremendous loss because they weren't prepared. They didn't do what it took because they weren't willing to put in the time or effort or find someone who would get the job done. Or they didn't think it could happen to them. They paid the price in the end and that's the ultimate lesson. I don't want you to experience that.

18. Be Yourself.

Another critical lesson of great leadership is to be yourself. Be who you were made to be. Do not try and fit into the mold of someone else or something else. Be yourself. No one likes imitators. The world doesn't need another Bob Dylan. It needs another unique, original voice. It doesn't need another Al Pacino. It needs another unique, original star. You need to be who you are and shine in the areas you shine brightest. You are absolutely supposed to learn from others. You should absolutely take and imitate the parts of others that you like and excite you. Those are necessary for success. But you are to be yourself.

19. Believe in God.

Believe in God's purpose for your life and live with love, laughter, joy, excitement and a desire to fulfill that purpose. Make sure the things you do have a positive impact on others. You will sleep well and be beloved if that is the case. As I shared previously, Erwin McManus said to me at dinner one night, "Why can't people just do what is good? There is so much opportunity to make money by doing good." At the end of the day I truly believe that motivated successful people can be successful at anything they set their minds to. I say that without bragging, but I have proven that in my own life. I was not a success at everything, but I was a success at most things. I applied the discipline, attitude, and concepts I have learned over the years to any situation I approach.

20. It's important to know when you're beaten.

It is important to know when a particular game is not for you. There could be a great party going on, but you don't like any of the people there. They're not your type. Let's say you're a sports guy and it's all tech people at the party. Let's say you're a tech guy and it's all music people at the party. It's just not your cup of tea or not your thing. Obviously, you're not going to have a passion for it. That's probably the wrong party for you and certainly the wrong one for you to stay at!

The same holds true in life, we have to break down the things we apply ourselves to in life. I truly believe you can be successful at anything you set your mind to. It's the type of person you are. It's the mentality of the person to succeed in what they do and to have the drive, passion, and desire to learn as well as the willingness to get ahead. Do what it takes, and be willing to do it well with excellence.

However, with that said, it is more critical to be able to do things you enjoy and love to do that will ignite your passion a hundredfold. They will pique your interest, excitement, desire to learn, and willingness to do what it takes. So you should be in businesses and working on stuff that excites you, fascinates you, and interests you. Just to be clear, you may not love everything you do. But, for the most part, you should love the field and the industries you're working in.

I don't think there's one particular thing you've got to be stuck in, but I do think in life sometimes we find ourselves in places and just accept the fact that we've been placed there. We do our best there. Sometimes that's not always the way to go. It is worth finding out what you love and pursuing it with passion at all cost.

Remember, it is your life. You have one life, one career, one time around the track on this Earth. Go and do it, and you might as well get the most out of it. Enjoy it and be as accomplished and successful as possible. Impact the world for great things and most importantly, the most important lesson I could ever teach you, is to enjoy the ride. Enjoy the ride along the way. It's not about later. It's about now.

You want to have passion and excitement. You want to be around people who are exciting and passionate, and who will inspire, encourage, and motivate you. You, in turn, will motivate them. Having a common goal is critical. That is why I believe you can succeed at anything you put your mind to if you have that attitude.

I think I have a unique eye for looking at things and seeing opportunity, a real desire for enjoyment, and for success and for excitement because I like those things. I have a unique desire to impact people for the better and see them have better lives, a unique desire to pour into people with what I learned, no matter what the subject is. But you know what? I learned from people as I went. I took the time and invested to learn. Mr. Bewkes was right. There is no shortcut, but that's okay. The good news is you can still get there. The bad news is there is still no shortcut.

So, if you want to get there, I suggest you go down the road and do what it takes. Keep moving forward on your path to success.

START NOW!

TAKE ACTION

* Start now. Start today. You can be successful, but there are no shortcuts.

* Review what we've talked about, make the appropriate changes and modifications in your life, and get going!

ENDING THOUGHTS

I hope I've been able to help you and be a blessing to you. I hope some of the experiences I've gained will translate into knowledge and wisdom in your life. I hope you won't have to learn some of the lessons I've learned the hard way, but will take them to heart and apply them immediately. I know they work.

This book was about the most important business and career lessons I've learned and so I've kept it focused on business. In case you care to know, some of the greatest life lessons I've learned and by far the greatest wisdom, knowledge and blessing I've ever seen or experienced, and what has helped me live an unbelievably fulfilling, joyful and productive life have come from the truth, knowledge and wisdom that God has shared with me. If you want the true treasure in life, that's where you'll find it.

Below is a motivational quote from the Bible I really love. Do this and your life will definitely have a positive impact on others!

Matthew 5:16 "Let your light so shine before men, that they may see your good works, and glorify your Father which is in heaven."

God Bless You

Jack

SPECIAL THANKS

My wife Beth. Honey, I no longer measure our marriage by how many years we've been together but by how many books we've survived through! Thank you for your patience and letting me do whatever I want to do. Trust me, you cannot put a price on that! I love you! Let's keep the train rolling!

I have 3 wonderful children—My youngest Jackson and Talia. I hope you will both read this book and these lessons will impart wisdom that will benefit you and bless you for the rest of your life. There is no one I'd rather see impacted by these truths and lessons than my children.

To my oldest Ricky, (and Kristi and Harper) Ricky, I believe I already taught you everything I know, so while you may not know the names and stories in this book you probably recognize many of the lessons already. The great news for you as a father is not only do you get to share the lessons in this book if you choose to teach them to your daughter, but you also get to teach her your own life lessons and the important things you have learned. Kristi, I know you will have many of your own lessons to share with Harper as well. She is a very lucky girl. I love you guys so much.

Mom. I learned so much from you about so many things in life not mentioned in this book. They could surely fill another book. Things like how to love, how to care about others, putting others above and before yourself, kindness, compassion, sharing and unconditional love. You have always been the greatest mom and still are!

Dad. Thanks for all the great lessons not just in business but in life! Thanks for always being there for me. You always were and still are the greatest.

My brother and his awesome family. Mike, Leslie, Dylan and Zac—Mike I have learned many lessons from you, boy... and I appreciate all of them... many in life and in business. I am lucky to have a brother like you who is always there for me. Like you told the lady behind the cash register at Sbarro's Pizza the night we went to see Springsteen On Broadway when she asked if we are paying together or separate... you said "together forever, until the end". Leslie, Dylan and Zac, you are among the kindest, most caring, loving people I have ever met... the fact that I am related to you and get the hang out with you all my life makes it even better!

Amanda Brown. Amanda, you are a great editor and your insight is truly invaluable to me. Your keen, sharp ability to keep me on track and provide valuable suggestions and critical input is worth more than you can ever know! Most of all I've appreciated getting to know you over the years. Even though it's long distance and by e-mail and phone, you are a valued friend and a trusted loyal editor. It is my privilege and pleasure to continue to pray for you and your family.

Shaun Smith. Well, brother, you lived long enough to see more books. Thank you for taking the time to invest in me personally and doing whatever I ask you to do! I know sometimes I pushed the limit and I'm sure your patience as well. But I so much appreciate the fact that you have never given me one bit of aggravation or push-back. You just always responded with humbleness, compassion and love, always offering to help me... no matter how stressful of a burden it was for you. I just want you to know I truly appreciate it. I put a tremendous value on your time and effort, and I do not take for granted all the help you've given me with my books and ministry through the years. You are a wonderful blessing. To God be the glory.

John Rabe. As always, brother, you delivered again. I appreciate your insight and wisdom. You have brought blessing and excellence to every project I've asked you to help on. You have a keen eye that leads you to give me just the right insight, analysis and input I need for each project. I assume the Holy Spirit is directing you (because no one could be that good on their own... Smile!) I'm truly grateful for you and your friendship and the blessing you've been to my life

Keith Greiveldinger. I know you're a busy man... your career and all those kids running around the house, but I really appreciate you taking time to read through the book and offer your comments and insights. You bring a unique perspective to the world and I truly appreciate your insight and time. Thank you for investing in me, brother.

Scott Wolf. Well buddy, this is getting old hat making covers for books and doing interior design. I think this is our third one together. The good news for me is they just keep getting better and better. I hope you're having more fun with each one. I know I drive you crazy as I keep changing things even after I tell you were are done. Smile! But I hope and believe that we both agree with the results—books that impact and influence people's lives for the better and for the kingdom of God! Thank you for your help. It is greatly appreciated. More than that I value your friendship, which is the true treasure for me.

All the wonderful business and career people who have influenced and impacted me—many of them are mentioned in this book—and to all those who aren't, I thank you as well. You have all impacted and influenced me for the better, and I have learned from all of you. While over the years there have been too many of you to mention individually, each one of you has a special place and page in my heart and mind! Thank you.

Also to my wonderful friends and family at Purpose Church Orlando. My family and I are blessed to have and be part of such a loving and caring church family.

All the awesome and inspirational brothers at IronMen of God men's ministry, and the local pastors here in Central Florida who have been such a blessing to me, thank you I appreciate it so much.

My friend and brother Sean LaGasse whose vision and inspiration was the genesis and birth of Purpose Church Orlando and who I have the pleasure of being involved with in both church and business.

Pastor George Cope and my Tuesday morning Bible study group for all the awesome bible teaching and fellowship! You guys are awesome!

Pastor Truman Herring and my friends and family at Boca Glades Church who have loved me and inspired for so many years.

Pastor Rob Taylor and Pastor Mike Butzberger for supporting my hopes and dreams since the beginning.

Joseph Patton and all the other college professors and teachers who have let me speak to their marketing, advertising, management, TV production and entrepreneurial classes. Thank you for giving me the privilege of impacting future generations. It is one of my greatest blessings.

CHECK OUT

LIVE A LIFE THAT MATTERS FOR GOD

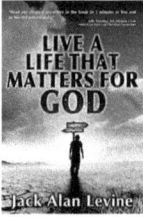

"From a clinical perspective, *Live a Life That Matters for God* has great value as a teaching and therapeutic tool for the soul. From a spiritual perspective it is a direct hit right to the heart of every Christian. This uplifting book will inspire you no matter what chapter you are reading. I love that you can pick up any chapter, anywhere, in any section in the book and be blessed immediately. Jack covers so many different topics that are relevant and critical to our growth as Christians, our happiness and our desire to walk closer with God. Jack's style is straight to the point and laser focused. Jack doesn't just tell you to do it, he shows you how!"

Julie Woodley,

MA, Division Chair American Assoc. of Christian Counselors

WHERE THE RUBBER MEETS THE ROAD WITH GOD

For every believer who wants to make sure they hear "Well done good and faithful servant."

"A knock out punch for Jesus if there ever was one. Jack Alan Levine's book is the heavyweight champion of the world when it comes to Christians walking a life of faith with God. Read it and make certain you will wear the champion's crown of life for Christ."

Nate "Galaxy Warrior" Campbell,

3x Lightweight Champion Of The World

DON'T BLOW IT WITH GOD

In *Don't Blow It With God*, Jack Levine reveals his road map to discovering God's blueprint for living the ultimate Christian life each and every day. Come along for the ride as God teaches Jack life-changing lessons that will help you in your life journey. Jack discovers how to live an abundant Christian life experiencing true joy, peace and happiness and along the way you will discover the formula and the insights about how you can too.

"Jack's unique style of communicating God's plan for an abundant life is a must read for all Christians. This book knocks it out of the park. If you've been striking out and want your life to be the perfect game for God then you need to read this book."

Chris Hammond, Major League Baseball pitcher

MY ADDICT YOUR ADDICT

This book is about addiction. Author Jack Levine has counseled thousands of people over the years who have gone through addiction, and knows what a torturous life it can be to be caught up in it. It's an awful thing.

He's experienced addiction in his own life and as a parent, as he watched his son struggle with addiction for years (it started when he was 18).

Whether you are in the throes of addiction yourself or seeing a loved one suffer through it, this book can help you. Jack has results and solutions for real-life situations. Each person's situation is different, but the root is the same for everybody. Through his own story, he can tell you what the choices are, the impacts of those choices, the results of those choices, and what sacrifices you'll have to make to get where you want to be.

PIECES STILL GOOD

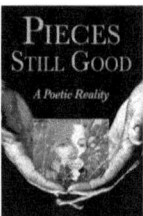

His writings emanate from questions like Who am I? What is the purpose of life? As well as the suffering, pain, realizations, romantic breakups, and uncertainty regarding the course of his future. Jack's intense feelings are reflected in his poetry. Although not all of it was pleasant and he is embarrassed by some of these writings, Jack publishes them all, unedited, leaving nothing out, so you truly walk with him through this phase of his life. There was torment, confusion, frustration, dissatisfaction, fear, and greed, along with a host of other feelings... And then a transition to a better way of life- a life filled with peace, joy, hope, happiness, mercy, love, and kindness. Jack's goal is to inspire his readers, make them think, and most importantly serve as an example.

JACK'S OTHER BOOKS...

DOWNLOADING GOD

"*Downloading God* is the file of information that today's generation needs to click on more than ever. Jack Levine's authentic and transparent self-disclosure rings through in his passionate devotion to his Lord and Savior Jesus Christ. His simple, straightforward, trademark writing style as in his previous books allows the reader to easily absorb, appropriate and apply the word and truth of God in a realistic, revolutionary and redemptive way. 'Downloading God' has short chapters all themed around a clever computer technology motif which makes the timeless truths of God both real and relevant to contemporary culture."

Dr. Jared Pingleton, VP American Association of Christian Counselors,
Clinical Psychologist, Credentialed Minister

TIME GONE

Each year we like to send a holiday letter to our friends and loved ones looking back at the past year and looking forward to the coming one. These letters are extremely personal but also extremely universal. Though written at holiday time, the observations I share are a true reflection of life all year long. In them I share my struggles, joys and thoughts, which like yours, change from year to year and I'm sure mirror many of the same things you go through.

I've left some personal things in here to give you a sense of who I am - a regular person like you with all the normal victories, defeats, happiness, sadness, joy and pain that we all share. Each letter contains reflections, lessons learned, wisdom and insight that God laid on my heart that particular year. I believe these will help you with your life and have great value to you. In these annual holiday letters I ask people to stop, take stock of where they were at, and consider how they were going to move forward. I hope that by sharing these letters with you it will cause you to do the same.

THE MOTIVATED LIFE

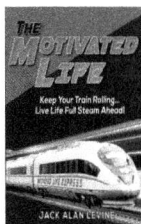

What powers your train? You know, some are powered by steam and some by diesel. Some are powered by electricity, and others are powered by battery. Some are even powered by solar energy. But, one thing's for sure. The train needs power to run, and so do you in your life.

So, what powers your train in life? Is it passion and purpose? Is it survival, money, or accomplishment? Is it fear? Perhaps fear of loss? Fear of missing out? It's very important to know what powers you, what motivates you, and what drives you forward each day. And, it's very important to have something that does all of these things. The more powerful your train, the faster and farther you can go and the quicker you can get there.

"It will encourage and accelerate you! Enriches, equips and inspires you to get the most out of every are of your life. I wholeheartedly recommend it."
Peter Lowe
President & Founder Peter Lowe International Get Motivated, Success Seminars

LEARN MORE ABOUT JACK

JackAlanLevine.com

www.ingramcontent.com/pod-product-compliance
Lightning Source LLC
Chambersburg PA
CBHW070724220326
41598CB00024BA/3282